You Only Feel We
When You're Out of the Water

Thoughts on Psychology
and Competitive Swimming

by
Dr. Keith Bell

Library of Congress Cataloging-in-Publication Data

Bell, Keith F.
    You only feel wet when you're out of the water /
    by Keith F. Bell.
        p.   cm.
    ISBN 0-945609-15-9: $16.95
    1. Swimming—Psychological aspects. I. Title.
GV838.53.P75B48   1991
797.2'101'9—dc20   *91-3321*
                                                      CIP

Portions of this book appeared originally in *Swimmers Magazine*, *SWIM SWIM*, and *SWIM Magazine* in different form.

Cover photograph by Sandy Neilson-Bell.
Cover: Keena Bell

Printed in the United States of America.

10 9 8 7 6 5 4 3 2

This book is available at a special discount when ordered in bulk quantities.

Published and distributed by:
KEEL PUBLICATIONS
P.O. Box 160155
Austin, Texas 78716

for Sandy,

who flows through life with the same beauty and grace
with which she glides through the water

Table of Contents

Preface

On a table in my office lies a binder filled with articles and columns I have written over the years for *Swimmers*, *SWIM SWIM*, *SWIM* and other magazines. Many of the athletes who seek my counsel pick it up and start reading. I'm always glad that they are interested in what I have to say. Besides feeling flattered, I most often find it easier and more efficient to work with athletes who have gotten a head start by reading some of what I have written. Through my writing and their reading we plow some common ground and acquire a common language with which to further explore the issues that bring them to me in the first place; those that revolve around the pursuit of athletic excellence.

Although I am frequently asked to lend out this binder, I never do so. It is one of the four things in this world that I never lend out: this binder, my goggles, my fins and my wife. Like the others, it is not easily replaced. Besides, it gets a lot of use in my office.

Every time I reread one of the articles I wrote, I discover areas in which I have grown or my thoughts have evolved. Then I want to change what I had written and share my growth, rethinking, and newly discovered ideas with other swimmers and coaches. At the same time, I frequently rediscover the applicability of ideas and techniques of which I had written years ago. Then I want to share what I hope will be of use to the swimmers and coaches who might have missed the magazines and to remind those who have read these articles, but who might benefit from rediscovery as do I, of the issues and techniques described. But I don't want to lend out my binder. And not everyone can visit my office. Thus, the birth of this book.

You Only Feel Wet When You're Out of the Water is a collection of some of my thoughts about psychology and competitive swimming. *You Only Feel Wet When You're Out of the Water* contains essays written expressly for this book; some never before published works; and many previously published columns and articles, most of which I have reworked, several of them substantially.

Swimmers magazine was directed at age group competitive swimmers, *SWIM SWIM* magazine was, and *SWIM* magazine is, directed at masters competitive swimmers and adult fitness swimmers. As a result, the columns I wrote for these magazines were aimed at these respective audiences. This I haven't changed. I don't think the level at which I have directed my comments will matter to you. It has always been my feeling that masters swimmers can learn much from the kids and that younger swimmers, from novice to elite, have a tremendous amount to learn from the masters. So too are the challenges facing each similar, if not identical.

My column for *SWIM SWIM* magazine took a question and answer form. I have chosen to leave these articles in that form, even when substantially rewritten.

The essays contained in *You Only Feel Wet When You're Out of the Water* appear in no particular order, with a few exceptions. I intentionally placed a couple of the articles regarding thinking skills toward the front. They will be useful in reading many of the other essays. I also placed the papers on commitment and attitude near the beginning, in the hope that they will mold the reader's view of other issues. With these thoughts in mind, feel free to skip around and read whatever title may catch your interest.

As in my books, *The Nuts and Bolts of Psychology for Swimmers, Winning Isn't Normal, Target on Gold: Goal Setting for Swimmers and Other Kinds of People,* and *Coaching Excellence,* I have striven to make *You Only Feel Wet When You're Out of the Water* readable to even the young age-grouper. That's not to say however, that the issues are easy to resolve or that the techniques are in any way simple to master or apply. They are not. I have chosen my words carefully, for the psychology of performance enhancement requires that language be precise. What we think and say, and how we think and say it, makes all the difference in the world. I hope you will carefully attend to, and apply, what you read.

So too, may some of the essays be read on different planes. "The Self-Image Fairy Tale," for example, is a young swimmer's story, a how-to essay, and a scathing criticism of self-image psychology all rolled into one. Use it and enjoy it on whatever level(s) you choose.

I hope you will find *You Only Feel Wet When You're Out of the Water* thought provoking and fun to read. Most of all, I hope *You Only Feel Wet When You're Out of the Water* helps you to swim faster, to better enjoy your swimming, and to win your races (unless, of course, you are swimming against Sandy, Kirsten, Keena, Bridger, Cooper, or me).

I'll see you around the pool.

You Only Feel Wet
When You're Out of the Water

Things are not always what they seem. Certainly, our language doesn't always help us think clearly and rationally. Our perceptions often do us disservice. Common knowledge is frequently wrong; prevailing wisdom often foolish.

Have you ever noticed that you only feel wet when you are out of the water? Think about it. When do you feel wet? Do you feel wet when you are completely submerged, streamlining through the water? I don't. I don't have the slightest awareness of being wet, when I'm underwater.

Do you feel wet when you are standing on the deck, having just climbed out of the water? I do, dripping wet, especially if there is a breeze. Does that mean that air makes you wet? Or does air just make you feel wet? Or, maybe, wind just makes you feel wetter? But doesn't the breeze dry you off?

How about when you are standing waist-deep in the water? Do you feel wet from the waist up or from the waist down? I don't know about you, but I only feel wet on those parts of my body that are out of the water. Of course, the parts that feel wet to me are those parts that have been in the water, but are no longer. If I'm standing waist-deep in the water, having already been totally submerged, my upper body, which is now out of the water, feels wet. On the other hand, if I'm standing waist-deep in the water, not yet having submerged my upper body, I feel dry from the waist up.

What do you feel from the waist down in this situation? I don't feel dry from the waist down, but I don't feel wet either. I guess the frame of reference changes. Wet is not of issue. My pelvis and legs feel cold, warm, or refreshed, depending upon the temperature of the water.

What if you dare to touch someone else? Does he feel wet to you if you touch him underwater? Nah!

Does someone else feel wet to you if you touch him when he is out of the water? Yes, I guess so, but only if he has been in the water. And, here's the kicker, only if you are dry.

If you are wet and you touch someone else who is wet, do you feel wet, except where you touch them? Do they feel wet except where being touched? Does your wetness merge?

Ah, but does someone else feel wet to you if they have just now climbed out of the water and you are wet? For that matter, if you feel wet, having recently been in the water, but being out now, and you touch someone who is dry, do they feel wet? Do they become wet? Do you become dry?

Or is this whole thing all wet? Have I dampened your enthusiasm, or merely whet your appetite? I know one thing: I feel all wet when I've been out of the water too long. Swimming brings me life. It brings me sustenance. But then, only a swimmer can know how wet it can feel to be out of the water.

Commitment

You're tired, stressed out, hungry, feeling drained, you have no goals in sight, and — THE WATER IS COLD. You've managed to make it into your suit and onto the deck, but getting into the water is a whole other matter. There isn't even any internal dialogue on the question as to when (or whether or not) you will actually get into the water. You merely feel the tug-of-war going on inside; a battle that pulls in both directions, leaving you frozen in an almost trance-like inertia.

Eventually, you make it to the water's edge. There, three or four times, you muster some movement toward diving in; movement that is internally perceptual, but functionally nonexistent. Finally, you break through the internal conflict with a subvocal imperative commanding the sudden, forceful leap needed to shatter your inertia. Your body lifts upward into the air, cutting an arc toward the cool, clear liquid below and the awaiting training session. Only now, as you reach the peak height of your dive, do you realize that your commitment is total. There are no more decisions to be made. You are getting into the water.

You've decided that you are going to swim. Nevertheless, how many times do you reevaluate that decision in the face of an early morning alarm, the feelings accompanying the end of a stressful day, an invitation to go out to dinner or cold water? Not that sleeping-in, dining out, finding some other way to unwind, or keeping warm are bad. It's just that opting to skip your swim effects future decisions. One such decision leads to two and two lead to twelve. Then it becomes much harder to build any consistency into your training and subsequently more difficult to reach whatever goals you might have set. Besides, you've already decided that you are going to swim. Why raise an issue that has already been resolved?

Without commitment, behavior fluctuates. There is always something else to do besides swimming. Moreover, many of the activities on the infinitely long list of competing alternatives are attractive. Lacking commitment, as each opportunity presents itself, you are faced with deciding whether or not to swim.

Swimming is great fun. And, as you well know, beyond enjoyment, swimming holds much promise. The fulfillment of that promise however, demands at least a modicum of consistency of training; consistency that is threatened, if you decide on your day's activities one day at a time without regard for your long-term goals. For it is the *collective* value of training that brings the sought-after rewards of health, weight control, muscle tone, and competitive excellence. One training session lost or gained matters not so much in isolation. That practice's place in the collection of training however, matters tremendously. Thus, the importance of making the decisions that collectively determine your action over time in a wide variety of circumstances: commitment.

The Random House Dictionary defines commitment as a pledge or promise. I like to think of commitment as a decision. To me, commitment is a big decision to make a lot of little decisions to take goal-oriented action. As such, it obviates the need to make the same decisions over and over again at different times, in various situations, or under diverse conditions. Commitment is a decision that relieves the burden of needlessly processing megabytes of input and of chronically re-assessing values and priorities in order to make decisions that have already been made. Commitment funnels action through everyday distractions and protects against the shortsighted choice of competing alternative action that only hinders long-term reward.

With a commitment to your swimming you know you want to do it. You are not forced to choose over and over again to swim. You've already decided to swim. When committed to your swimming you tend not to ask yourself those otherwise recurring rhetorical questions: "Do I want to do this?" "Why am I doing this?" and "Why am I here?" You know why.

There's an old proverb that points out that even a journey of a thousand miles begins with but a single step. That first step is often difficult to take. If you make each step as hard-earned as the first one, any journey becomes slow and arduous. If each prospective step invokes thoughts questioning the wisdom of such action ("Should I take this step? I may fall and hurt myself. I may get tired. I may bypass some excitement right here."), each decision could be overwhelming. What a chore to have to overcome such conflict prior to taking each step. How will you ever get where you are going? You may never do anything. Moreover, such chronic re-evaluation and decision making detract from the fun. The flow is interrupted. How much easier and more pleasant it is to glide though your journey unencumbered by the burdens of assessing the value and cost of each individual step.

Just as so many of you, for various reasons, I've decided to swim. For me however, whether or not I swim is rarely at issue. The question for the day, should one arise at all, is more likely to spring from among: "Where will I swim?" "What time will I swim?" "What type of training do I want to do?" and "How far will I swim?" As a result, I haven't missed a day in the water in over three years. Some days I rest: I may only swim easy for a few hundred yards, but I get in. It's a nice part of the day, one to which I look forward and enjoy. There's no decision to be made. I'm commited.

Similarly, though the exact nature of my training commitment varies with the time of season and from season to season with my goals, I make a commitment to putting in at least some specified amount of yardage. Usually my commitment calls for at least 4,000 yards at least four days per week, and an unspecified minimum for the other three. You may want to commit yourself to three to four swims per week. Seven days per week is not for everyone. So too, will your concept of optimal yardage likely differ from mine.

Of course, the higher the level of excellence to which you aspire, the greater your level of commitment needs to be. Regularly swimming a certain amount of yardage should help you to maintain a good, healthy level of fitness, but competitive excellence requires much more. Goals set to train at least as fast as certain specified speeds, to lift at least some specified minimum amount of weight on particular weight training drills, or to streamline past the flags, for example, map the steps in your journey. Commitment to such goal-directed action keeps you on track. More ambitious goals require greater levels of commitment.

Whatever your level of commitment, monitoring your commitment will help you to steer a steady course and to avoid remaking decisions that have already been made. Notations on a calendar provide clear feedback as to your level of commitment. I tend to track each day's yardage, as well as significant sets and times, on my calendar.

Log books may also be beneficial to those who do not find them too burdensome. Self-monitoring of this sort provides a basis for accurate evaluation concerning whether or not your swims meet your predetermined standards. This self-evaluation in turn tends to trigger self-reward or self-punishment that can profoundly influence how often, how far, how intensely, and how fast you swim.

Certainly any commitment that brings joy and consistency to one's swimming is valuable. Inconsistency erodes the benefits to be derived from our great sport.

Make a commitment to your swimming. Your commitment need not be all-consuming. It can be to swim at whatever frequency, duration, distance, and intensity you deem to be practical, rewarding and enjoyable. But make your commitment strong. Relieve yourself of the burden of internal battles you cannot win. Free yourself to flow unencumbered through the waves of your competitive swimming experience.

The tunes from my radio alarm clock wake me at 5:35 a.m. I'm tired. But without hesitation, I slowly reach over and turn off the soft music. Swinging out of bed, I step into my two bathing suits, climb into sweats and slip on my down boots. The morning air is cold and so am I. I grab a towel and my gear. I hop into the car and make the eight-minute drive to Jim's house.

As I pull up, Jim has already rolled the cover off of his one-lane, 25 yard, backyard pool and is busy vacuuming up last night's accumulation of sow bugs. I set my pull buoy, paddles, fins, and kick board at the side of the pool, synchronize the pace clocks, and place one clock at each end of the pool.

With six a.m., I leap to dive into the 68 degree water. Hovering in midair, I smile inwardly once again at this most poignant example of true commitment. Decisions are no longer significant. Gravity has taken over. There's no turning back. I am getting in.

Playing Swimming

When I grow up, I want to be a professional swimming player. That is, if I ever grow up. I hold dear the philosophy that you are only young once, but you can be immature all your life.

It always gets to me when I hear swimmers or coaches talking about "working out." Why is it that we play baseball, we play tennis, we play football, we play golf, we play basketball, we play frisbee, we play soccer, but when it comes time to swim, we *"workout"*?

"Workout" — now that sounds like work. I don't *"workout."* Neither do my teams. I practice, I train, but mostly I play swimming. Oh, I play intensely, but I play. Intense play is a fun part of the game. I love the challenge. No wonder swimming is such a nice time of the day.

By playing swimming instead of *"working out,"* I also tend to remain cognizant of the fact that meets are games. So too, am I reminded to keep training fun.

No, I don't want to go "workout." But I'm always up for a good game of swimming. I love to play swimming.

You see, the way that you think about your swimming (and, for that matter, the way that you talk about your swimming) has such a personal impact. You can't afford to be casual about your choice of words.

The language of our thoughts is the medium through which we sort out a complex world and bring it meaning. As such, language plays a major role in determining what we do and how we feel.

Words are the units of language. Unfortunately, people are often careless with the words they use to express their thoughts. Then, though the words loosely convey the intended meaning, the literal meaning is a distortion or exaggeration of the intended expression. Such casual expression can deter performance excellence, for we tend to take ourselves literally.

Choose your words carefully. They shape the meaning of your world. Take care to express yourself in a manner that best promotes enjoyment and excellence of competitive swimming.

Let's take a look at some other common examples of the effects of a poor choice of words:

The ineffable "**can'ts**":

> "I *can't* make this set."
> "I *can't* swim fly."
> "I *can't* beat Joe."

Often when you say I *"can't,"* it seems harmless. Usually, by *"can't,"* you mean that you are *having difficulty*, you *haven't recently*, you *haven't yet*, or you *don't think you will right now*. At least, if challenged, you probably would say you didn't really mean you are incapable of doing so: *you can't*. Rather, you probably would report that you meant one of the sentiments cited above, such meaning being consistent with the facts. But *"can't"* goes beyond those meanings, implying so much more and affecting what you do.

The word *"can't"* often limits, in advance, what you do, not because of accurately assessed capability, but by limiting your goals, your effort, or your very decision to act. Even if you don't literally mean that you *"can't,"* saying so subtly defines your capacity. Say (or think) you *"can't"* often enough and you begin to believe it. Then, since you know you can't anyway, you tend to approach challenges with a *"why try?"* attitude.

The irony lies in the fact that you never have any evidence that you cannot do something. I *"can't"* is never verifiable. It merely expresses belief, not fact. You can know that you have never before made a certain interval, posted a certain time, or defeated a certain opponent. But such history presents no proof of future limitations. Who knows what you may do at the next opportunity?

Your performance history isn't even a measure of what you were capable in the past. It only records what you did at a particular moment in time, under some particular set of circumstances. We have no proof that you could not, only that you did not. So why limit yourself?

What if, when you find yourself missing the interval, instead of thinking *" I can't make this interval,"* you thought, *"I'm having difficulty making the interval"*? What if, instead of thinking, *"I can't' beat Joe,"* you thought, *"I haven't beaten Joe recently"* or *" I've yet to beat Joe"*? Instead of despair you may invoke hope, determination, and subsequent goal-oriented, effortful action.

Hard — Of course, much of the physical preparation for the game is difficult. You want to compete at a high level of excellence. Physical adaptation takes place as a result of stressing your body. If preparation is easy, there can be little, if any, gains.

Yes, *"intense play"* can be difficult, especially if you set challenging goals. But isn't that what tough sets are — *"challenges"*? *"Hard"* sounds so cold and, well — hard. A *"challenge"* however, sounds exciting.

Have-to — If you *"have to"* do something, you tend to resist. If you *"have to"* train in order to perform well, then *"workouts"* tend to become necessary evils, the dues you must pay in order to swim fast.

If you *"want to"* train, then *"playing swimming"* is eagerly anticipated. The *"challenges"* of the game are fun and exciting. Each day's practice is enjoyable and valuable in, and of, itself. *"Playing swimming"* becomes an *"opportunity,"* not the *"obligation"* inherent in *"working out."* Then, swimming fast in meets is the icing on the cake. The trip is worthwhile regardless of the destination. Meanwhile, you become more free to commit yourself, to "let go" and "go for it" without concern of failure, because, in many ways, you have already won.

To be — The verb *"to be,"* in its various forms, can be truly problematic, especially when applied to your Self. It tends to define existence. When you say *"I am,"* even to yourself, it tends to put you in a nonchangeable box. It tends to limit your performance and your ability to change. If you think, *"I am lazy,"* *"I'm not a butterflyer,"* or the like, you tend to act to make it so (or, even more often, you make it so by failing to act). Yet, you are not lazy, even when you act as if you are. You can easily act differently.

You may think you aren't a butterflyer, but should you train to swim butterfly, who knows? You wouldn't be the first person to have their greatest success in what used to be his worst stroke. Ask one-time, butterfly world champion Joan Pennington.

The words you use to build your thoughts structure your world. They can build a highway to success or just form road blocks. Don't let the words get in the way.

Attitude Excellence

When someone tells you that you need to have a more positive attitude, what do you learn? Does such criticism teach you how to have a good attitude? It doesn't, does it?

I guess such a suggestion invites change, but what kind of change? Perhaps the call for a more positive attitude effectively points out what not to do. It lets you know what the critic deems as a bad attitude, doesn't it? But does it point out what your critic wants you to do?

Unfortunately, no one ever tells you how to have a good attitude. No one, that is, until now. I'm going to tell you how to exhibit a good attitude. Even more cogent, I'm going to tell you how to have a good attitude toward the pursuit of excellence in competitive swimming.

Attitudes reflect values. **A positive attitude is a manifestation of the high value you place on what you are doing.** A good attitude announces that you believe what you are doing to be good and worthwhile. A good attitude proclaims that you care about what you are doing and how well you do it.

A bad attitude reveals that you don't value your immediate pursuit. A bad attitude shows that what you are doing doesn't mean that much to you and that you don't particularly care how well you do it.

It's not that hard to exhibit a good attitude. You merely need to think, act, and talk as if what you are doing is good and worthwhile. That's easy — well, it's easy and it's hard. It's easy to label what you are doing as good and worthwhile and to act as if that is true, but it's hard to do so consistently.

It's not easy to consistently attend to the value in your activities. It's easy to be inattentive to the reasons for your undertaking and to lose your perspective; especially when what you do is out of habit or routine. When you do what you do because that's what time of day it is, it's easy to take your pursuits for granted and to fail to appreciate them at all.

It's easy to attend to the unattractive aspects of your routine and to let devaluing and derogatory comments and actions casually invade your behavior. It's easy to complain. Hell, everyone else does.

Our social systems work to support bad attitudes. Almost everyone else is ready to drag you down. It is socially acceptable to complain and devalue almost everything. It is not as socially acceptable, though surely more healthful, pleasant and functional, to praise the value of your pursuits.

Yet, in order to have a good attitude toward the pursuit of excellence in competitive swimming all you have to do is to act, think, and talk consistently with a philosophy that says:

**Competitive swimming is good. The more the better.
Challenges are good. The tougher the challenge, the better.**

If you act consistently with this philosophy, you will be approaching the challenges inherent in training and competition with a positive attitude. You'll be getting after it, relishing the game, and asking for more and tougher challenges.

Granted, I make some assumptions here. I assume that you have some reasons for swimming and that you find some value in it. But these are fair assumptions, are they not?

I also assume that if you are going to swim, for whatever reasons you chose to do so, you may as well value it and enjoy it. That too, is fair, isn't it? If so, having a good attitude makes sense.

Nevertheless, how many times have you heard yourself or others say: "What am I doing here?" or "Why am I doing this?"? How many times have you heard yourself or others say: "Coach, can we take a little extra rest here?" "Let's do fewer repeats." "How about longer rest intervals?" "Let's not go fly." "That's too hard." "I'm tired (in a tone that says being tired is bad) or "This set is boring." *Swimming is bad, more is worse.*

Comments such as those cited above only serve to make practices less pleasant and the pursuit of excellence more difficult. Even though you may not really mean these things when you say them (as evidenced by the fact that you are at practice, swimming), comments like these do take their toll on you and others around you.

It's hard enough to consistently demonstrate the high value you place on your swimming and on competitive excellence, without interference from others. Others tend not to help. You have to do it alone. Demonstrating a good attitude toward the pursuit of excellence in competitive swimming can be a lonely pursuit.

Others don't value what they do, let alone what you are doing. Others don't value excellence. They don't care if they do things well. They are content to wallow in mediocrity, but they don't want to do it alone.

Others are lazy, they are sloppy about what they do. They're not willing to do what it takes to excel and they don't want you to value excellence. They don't want to look bad in comparison.

Others don't value competition. Fear of poor performance is often temporarily dissipated, and feared challenges easily evaded, by devaluing the contest. Others don't want you to value competition. They don't like to get beat.

Peer pressure presents a serious threat to good attitudes toward competitive excellence. Peer pressure invites you to talk and act the same as everyone else, the same — average — mediocre! But you can't act the same as everyone else and excel. The very nature of excellence is superiority. To excel, by definition, is to outdo. Peer pressure pushes toward mediocrity.

Take warm-ups, for example. During warm-up most

swimmers are taking it easy, stretching it out, getting loose, and/or taking advantage of this portion of practice when speed is less emphasized by focusing on stroke technique. However, there often is one swimmer, who is ready to go and is getting after it from the moment he dives into the water. What usually happens? Another swimmer berates the eager swimmer with a "Slow down, it's only warm-up." The message sent: *Easy is good, challenges are bad.*

Or how about descend sets? Many of the practices I've encountered on various teams find almost everyone starting off easy and dropping five seconds per repeat, for example, throughout the set. Sometimes, there is one swimmer who really gets after that first repeat and attempts to descend from there. Inevitably, another swimmer calls out, "What are you doing? This is a descend set. The first one is supposed to be slow." Translated: *Easy is good, challenges are bad.*

What if you talked about the fun and the value of your swimming and asked for more and tougher? ("That was a good set." "That was fun." "Coach, can I go on a tougher interval and go every other one fly?" "Let's go 200s instead of 150s." In other words, *Swimming is good and more is better; challenges are good, the tougher, the better.*) What kind of attitude would you be exhibiting? What if everyone on your team talked like that in practice? What kind of atmosphere in which to train and compete would you create?

It isn't even necessary to start molding a more positive attitude with the more difficult aspect of attitude-change: thinking as if swimming is good and more is better and that challenges are good and the tougher, the better. (Though, challenges are good and the tougher, the better.) Merely acting as if the challenges inherent in the pursuit of competitive swimming excellence are good, and intentionally talking in a swimming-is-worthwhile vein will suggest a positive attitude and help to create one.

I know as a coach, I like to hear that my swimmers enjoy the practice and appreciate the opportunity. Even more important, I want them to pay attention to the fact that during practices they are where *they* want to be, pursuing their choice of activities because of the benefit they anticipate deriving from their swimming and the goals they seek to attain, and that they enjoy it. That's why, most often, in our practices the instructions for warm-down include directions for one: "Thanks, Keith. That was fun." This public acknowledgement of enjoyment and appreciation otherwise may not come spontaneously. When assigned however, such comments just as effectively draw attention to the value of training for competitive swimming and effectively build good attitudes.

So too, do intentionally performed acts and other planned comments work to prime attitudes. This is why, in my role as sports psychology consultant to so many teams, I often assign homework tasks designed to build good attitudes.

For example, a few years ago while doing a seminar for a team in Dallas, I assigned to all the swimmers the task of taking note of at least one thing they enjoy during the following morning's practice then commenting aloud about the fun. I told them that after identifying a swim, set, or drill that they liked, they could exclaim something like: "That was fun!" "That was great!" "I like that set!" or some other simply put comment.

The next morning I had to do some planning with the coach for the remainder of the seminar before I could train with the team. By the time I put on my swim suit and arrived on deck, the swimmers were just completing the warm-up. As I walked the deck toward the starting end of the pool, a high-schooler, Mike Heath, looked up at me, remembered his homework and loudly proclaimed, "Boy is this fun!" Everyone laughed. Another swimmer took Mike's cue and yelled, "Yeah, this is great!" More laughter.

During the remainder of practice, after almost each and every repeat, similar comments were directed to me, to the other swimmers, and generally announced. Meanwhile, everyone swam increasingly faster as the practice progressed and later reported that they thoroughly enjoyed themselves; all because one swimmer took the responsibility to perform a simple, assigned task.

Talk as if swimming is enjoyable, beneficial, and extremely valuable; act as if you like to swim and to tackle the challenges; welcome the challenges inherent in the pursuit of competitive swimming excellence. When you carelessly produce devaluing comments and thoughts, catch yourself and turn them around.

Value your swimming. You'll have more fun, get more out of it, and consistently contribute to our great sport with your good attitude.

Competitive swimming is wonderful. We all know it. Take care of it. To accept and joyfully tackle the challenges of competitive swimming excellence is exciting, exhilirating and just plain fun. Don't let anyone else tell you differently. You may be the only one around self-assured enough to show this positive attitude.

Dead Dog Meat

Have you ever had one of those days where you felt like "dead dog meat"? You know what I mean. You are so exhausted that you feel it in your bones.

It was one of those days. I had just stepped off a plane and was jet-lagged out. My business had been keeping me inordinately busy. I had been training extremely hard, especially with the weights. I dragged when I walked across the deck toward the water. Warm-up confirmed what my body had been telling me. I felt like "dead dog meat."

The Texas Swimming Center was set up long course meters. Warm-up was 16 times 50m. on the :40. I didn't make the interval. From there, my performance went downhill. We kicked a set consisting of eight fifties on the minute (descending one through four and five through eight), followed by four one hundreds descend on the two minutes and a 400m time trial. Rather, I should say that was the set, not that "we" kicked it. I didn't do the entire set. I didn't make the interval on the fifties. In fact, I only got six of them in prior to having to start on the hundreds. I didn't fare much better on the hundred repeats, finishing only three in the alloted time. The 400m. time trial was a 300 for me. I didn't want to hold up practice. That's how bad I felt. I didn't have anything. I felt like one giant moving sample of lactic acid.

From there our practice moved to a similar pull set. We pulled eight fifties on the :45 (descending one to four and five to eight), descended four one hundreds leaving on the 1:30 interval, and then went straight into a 400m. timed pull.

On top of everything else, I had been nursing a sore shoulder — a little bit of tendonitis. So, though everyone else in the pool was pulling with paddles and a tube, I opted to go without the tube.

Now, I generally pull much better than I kick anyway, but going tubeless gave me a competitive advantage. Even then, considering my sorry state, everyone must have been tired from the timed kick and must have been using the first couple of pulls as recovery swims, for as I pulled my fifties, I noticed that I was ahead of everyone else in the pool. Everyone, that is, except for one guy a few lanes over who was pretty much even with me on the fifty pulls. That guy being Rowdy Gaines, who at the time was the world record holder in the 100m. freestyle, American record holder in the 200yd. freestyle and a not-too-shabby 400 swimmer.

Descending through the four one hundred pulls, Rowdy and I pulled away from everyone else. Now, okay, I know that Rowdy has a tube on and I don't. But, hey — he's a world record holder and I'm about the same age as his father! So what if he's dragging some rubber around his feet and I'm unencumbered? I still thought it would be exciting to beat the world record holder. This was my chance.

I decided to take him in the 400m. timed pull. Now, I'm tough getting home. So I figured, I may be able to take him at the end, but I would need to stay with him going out. And I knew he wasn't going to wait around for me. So I sprinted the first 100. After all, this was a pull. I didn't think I'd totally wipe myself out doing that. I mean, I got after that first one hundred with all I was worth. And at the end of the first 100m. Rowdy was, oh — a body length ahead of me.

"Okay," I thought, "Rowdy's a little bit ahead, but I can get him at the end. He's not a distance swimmer. He's going to fade some. But I can't let him get too far ahead. I've got to be within striking distance."

So I sprinted the second hundred. Turning over as fast as I could, pulling with every ounce of power I could summon, I saved nothing for the end. I thought I'd worry about that later. Somehow, I'd find the strength to get it home. I kept Rowdy in my sights. As I came in to the fourth turn, he was, oh — two body lengths ahead of me.

Well, I wasn't going to give up. I was just going to have to go all out on the third hundred and hope I could reel him in. I remained determine to get him. Surely, he'd crater. I'd get him in the home stretch.

So I sprinted the third hundred. My arms screamed at me from within, but I payed no heed. My eyes just rivetted my attention on Rowdy. I wanted to beat him. I didn't know when I'd ever again get as good an opportunity. As I came into the sixth turn, Rowdy was, oh — about three body lengths ahead of me.

"Okay," I thought, "I can still get him. Maybe, he'll crash and burn." So I reached down deep and pulled out everything I didn't even know I had. I busted it every stroke of the way, driving to the finish.

I didn't get him. Rowdy finished, oh — about four body lengths ahead of me. But you know what? From a push, on a day when I felt like "dead dog meat," I pulled 400 meters within two seconds of my lifetime best, shaved and tapered time for the 400m. swim.

I don't know where that came from. I couldn't even make the intervals in any of the practice prior to that pull set. (And I wasn't cruising. I was giving it an honest effort.) Nor do I know where it went. For subsequent to that 400m. pull, I was worthless in practice. I couldn't even make the intervals on the rest of the repeats in practice.

I do know one thing. Whenever I don't feel as good as I'd like to feel in practice, and whenever I swim poorly in a race, I don't pronounce to myself that I don't have it. Rather, I remind myself of the time I felt like "dead dog meat" and I went after Rowdy Gaines.

Who knows when it may suddenly appear, even in the most unlikely of times? I want to be open to finding some speed, welcoming it with open arms, and taking advantage of the opportunity, no matter how unexpected a great swim may otherwise be.

I might have stunk up the pool on the last repeat or in the last race, but feelings of "dead dog meat" aside, this next one may still be outstanding. You just can't ever tell.

King of Zing

> *"You learn the pain in practice and you will know it in every race . . . at the threshold of pain, you have a choice. You can back off, or you can force yourself to drive to the finish, knowing the pain will become agony . . . Most swimmers back away from the pain but a champion pushes himself into agony."*
> — *Don Schollander*

One of the most formidable challenges facing every swimmer is the successful management of the painful sensations that accompany effortful performance. But you can learn to handle the pain. The key is to interpret the sensations accurately, and use them in a way that will best enable you to swim fast.

Pain is the body's warning signal. It alerts you that something biologically harmful is happening. Pain is an adaptive mechanism. We survive by learning to avoid anything potentially painful and by removing ourselves from situations where pain occurs. For example, if we ignored the pain we felt when we put a hand on a hot stove, considerable tissue damage would result. But by not touching hot stoves (or, at least, by quickly removing our hands when we feel the painful heat), we prevent (or minimize) burning our skin.

Precisely because it is so adaptive to do so, we learn early on that pain is bad and to avoid it. When we "hurt," the naturally acquired response is to stop what we are doing, to approach the activity tentatively, or to avoid it altogether. Generalizing our responses to being tired or to "hurting" when we swim, we tend to retreat from the source of the "pain" by easing up, slowing down, putting it on cruise control or we avoid it (skipping practice or scratching our races).

These responses don't always work. As Mark Twain put it, "Anyone who has touched a hot stove will never willingly touch one again; this is a wise response. But if he never will touch a cold one either, he is being foolishly cautious." Thus it is with swimming. You don't build strength or stamina and you don't win races by easing up when it starts to hurt, by merely flirting with the pain of effortful response or by avoiding the pain altogether. As is often said, "no pain, no gain."

Painful experiences teach caution, which is good. But they also make us overly careful and fearful of encountering any type of pain — which is bad, if we are swimmers.

Herein lies the challenge. We learn that pain is "bad." We don't like to hurt. We, quite adaptively, learn to fear pain and to unthinkingly act to avoid it. As a result our automatic reaction to pain is to retreat from it. But the self-inflicted "pain" of swimming is a necessary component of success. You want to swim fast. To do that "you gotta hurt."

Part of the problem stems from our language. We label a wide variety of vastly different sensations and experiences as painful. We say it "hurts" to be criticized, it's "painful" to lose, it "hurts" to swim ten two hundreds butterfly, it's a "pain" when someone in our lane won't let us pass. These "hurts" and "pains" are hardly the same. Nevertheless, because we say these experiences "hurt" us and think of them as "painful," we think they are bad, distasteful, and acts to be avoided if at all possible. The mere idea that something "hurts" brings forth associations of many other painful events thereby shaping our feelings and eliciting generalized responses: flight and avoidance. We tend to fail to limit our interpretation of the immediate sensations to the particular cause and type of pain. For that matter, we don't have much in the way of vocabularly available to help us to differenti-ate those sensations that warn us of danger from other intense sensations, even those that signal biological enhancement. We lump them all into the same "pain" box.

The "pain" of swimming is a fairly unique experience. Most non-athletes never experience sensations quite like those that swimmers entertain for hours daily. Non-athletes, and to some extent even non-swimmers who may be athletes, can't relate. (Try explaining to one of your friends what it feels like to really be getting after it in the water.) It is difficult to describe, but what you feel when swimming hard is definitely different than other kinds of pain. It's different in two ways: it signals different conse-quences, and it just plain feels different. The sensations you expe-rience while swimming signal adaptation: biological growth. Stress your body in the water, flirt with new speeds and longer duration of previously found speed, and you get faster, more pow-erful, and more biologically efficient. Meanwhile, the sensations you experience while accepting the challenge of training and com-petition are easily distinguished from those that signal actual or impending biological damage: true pain. Anyone who has ever swum with tendonitis, a pulled muscle, or even sore muscles knows that the sensations produced by swimming with injuries feels different than those generated by effortful performance.

True pain "hurts." The sensations signal real damage. The sensations may vary in intensity with the severity of the injury, but they are not all that qualitatively different.

Not so with the "pain" of swimming. The feelings of "pain" come more from our expectations of things labeled as "painful" and the way we talk about them ("coach, I died out there"), then they do from the actual sensations. As a result, the physical experience varies. Sometimes when you are loose and swimming fast, the "pain" of swimming feels good. It "hurts," but it's a good kind of hurt. It's exhilirating. Similarly, sometimes it doesn't seem to "hurt" much, or the "pain" is qualitatively dif-ferent — it doesn't seem "bad"; then it is easy to swim fast.

The converse is also true. When you are struggling to swim fast, the "pain" is exaggerated and seems so much worse. And when you are fighting the "pain," it is difficult to swim fast.

Fortunately, you can learn to manage the "pain." You can achieve "the good kind of hurt" more often. And you can learn to swim fast even when you are "hurting."

It is often said that people perceive pain differently due to different "pain thresholds." It is assumed that some people have low pain thresholds and feel pain from very slight injury, while others have high thresholds and feel pain only after intense injury. We know that in natural situations, people differ considerably in their subjective experience of pain and in their ability to tolerate it. The evidence from laboratory studies however, indicates that virtually all people experience a sensation at the same level of stimulus input. Clearly, except in rare instances where there exists some physical abnormality, differences in pain tolerance are largely psychological, not physiological.

Psychologically, the ability to tolerate pain, and to perform well in spite of it, depends on how you appraise the pain, to what you attribute the pain, and how you assess your ability to cope with it. If you see pain as something bad, it is more difficult to tolerate it. For that matter, if you assess something painful as being bad for you, which it most often is, it makes little sense to tolerate the pain if you can escape from it. Unfortunately, as previously mentioned, the idea that anything termed "pain" is bad and should be avoided is well ingrained, but the moment you label the sensations that accompany effortful performance as "pain" and therefore "bad," you tend to tighten up. This increased muscular tension further contributes to fatigue and serves to magnify the intensity with which these sensations are experienced, making it even more difficult to swim fast.

But you need not view the "pain" of swimming as something "bad." It's not. It's good. It signals adaptation. You can appropriately interpret the sensations as signals that you are building power, getting in shape, or expanding your body's capacity in a quest for swimming excellence.

Nor does "pain" need to be a signal to back off from the pressure. Easing up and slowing down when you "hurt" is an easily acquired habit, but it is a habit, not a necessary reaction. You can learn, instead, to use the "pain" as a signal to stay with it and even as a signal to pick it up. With practice, picking it up in response to the sensations accompanying effortful performance can become your habitual response. Eventually, you can get to the point where anytime you start to "hurt," you automatically pick up the pace.

Now that's not to say that muscle fatigue doesn't take it's toll, hampering your ability to swim fast. Obviously, it does. But we rarely get to the point where speed is diminished purely by the physiological effects of fatigue. Most often we lose it psychologically before we do physically. Viewing the "pain" as something bad and fearing it gets us slowing down before we need to and more than we need to.

To what you attribute the "pain" is another critical factor. If you think you are "hurting" because you took it out too fast, you "don't have it today," you are injured or otherwise lack the capacity to maintain a good pace, let alone if you think you are going to "die"; you are pushing the button to slow down. On the other hand, viewing the "pain" and fatigue as natural results of swimming hard helps you to stay relaxed and leaves the door open for you to maintain or increase your speed. By accepting these physical sensations as normal, instead of viewing them as horrible; you more easily read your body, adjust your pace, relax, and stretch out your stroke. Fear of "pain" tends to make you tighten up, "crater," and get into trouble.

If you experience the "pain" as something horrible (essentially, if not explicitly, likening it to "dying"), then you begin to wonder how much longer you can keep it up, or you may even decide right then that you can't take it any longer: as if, since you could no longer take it, if you kept up your effort, you would actually expire; you'd die. I guess it is conceivable for someone to extend himself beyond his physical capacity, putting such a strain on his body that it ceases to function, but, especially for a highly conditioned athlete, this seems unlikely. Let's face it, people don't die from swimming fast. The body has too many built-in protective mechanisms. Someone might die while swimming because of some genetic defect, but that's different. It is not from swimming fast. If you are overextending yourself, you get different sensations, ones you should heed as should you heed the warnings of any true "pain." Herein, we are talking about a different kind of pain. You know the difference. Swimmers must learn to distinguish between harmful and helpful "pains." True "pain" is a warning that must be heeded before greater damage is done.

Of course, you don't consciously slow down because you really think the "pain" you are experiencing is going to kill you. As we've seen, slowing down in response to the "hurt" is a habit developed spurring you to act as if you thought this way. More than likely, when you do slow down, it is not because you can't take the "pain" — it's never that bad — rather, your decreased effort probably stems from doubts as to your ability to continue to tolerate pain that you think might keep getting worse. So you bail out before finding out that it never gets so bad.

The real conceptual difficulty is understanding that the only thing that makes it feel bad is calling it "pain." "Pain" is bad and feared. Sensations called pain must "hurt." Anything that "hurts" must feel bad. The truth is however, that the sensations you experience when swimming hard are merely intense sensations; intense sensations signaling impending adaptation. They don't need to feel bad or to "hurt." They only "hurt" because you think they "hurt." They could easily be experienced as interesting and, perhaps, even pleasurable.

Admittedly, these sensations are discomforting. Building speed and stamina requires extending yourself beyond the limits of physical and psychological comfort. But a lot of experiences in life are discomforting, yet quite exhilirating; skiing, riding a roller coaster, watching a good suspense thriller at the movies, sex, and swimming, for example. In each of these instances, the intense sensations accompanying each activity, can be, and often is, experienced as pleasurable. The sensations experienced are clearly not comfortable, they are discomforting, but they are not "pain." Anyway, what's so great about comfort? Comfort is boring.

When it starts to "hurt," take it one stroke at a time. Don't get ahead of yourself and don't catastrophize about pain and resulting biological damage that realistically won't occur. Relax. Remind yourself that the "pain" is not so bad. You can take it. And tell yourself that you can handle it as it comes. It is not intolerable. In fact, it is the anxiety over potential unpleasantness that is hard to tolerate. Even better, welcome the discomfort. Remind yourself that it can feel interesting, good, or even exhilirating and pleasurable if you let it.

Relaxation is a major step in pain management. The more you relax while you swim, the less energy you burn, the more you delay fatigue, and the less intensely you experience the "pain." Relaxation keeps you calm. When relaxed, you worry less about "hurting" and you don't panic at the perception of fatigue. When relaxed, you are more likely to accept the sensations, to view them as good, and perhaps even embrace them.

Use the sensations as signals to relax, stay loose, and pick it up. We talk too much about "pushing through the pain." This implies fighting against yourself, which creates muscular tension and exaggerates any discomfort. Don't push through; loosen up and swim *with* the feeling of effort. Think relaxed speed.

The real key to handling the "pain" of swimming fast is to stop seeing it as something bad to be feared, avoided or from which to retreat. View these sensations as being positive, make them your allies — signals that you are training or competing hard, building power, gaining stamina, and swimming fast.

Remember that the "pain" that accompanies effortful swimming is different than the pain of injury or illness. It is not a warning of physical harm. It is the natural result of exercising your body. Accept the sensations as part of what you are doing. They don't have to be scary or bad if you read the sensations as signals of adaptation. What's so bad about biological growth? It only enhances your capacity for speed.

The best thing you can do is to stop calling it "pain." True pain is a signal of impending or actual biological damage. The "pain" of swimming is not. Calling it pain is psychologically confusing. As Lothar Kipke, the G.D.R. National Team physician, told me, "There is no pain in swimming. Pain is when they [swimmers] are sick or injured. Pain is bad. Sports are fun. They never go together."

You are better off referring to the sensations with a term that brings forth more positive associations. A few years ago, when I was discussing "pain" management with his Montclair Swim Team, Coach Steve Haufler suggested the term "zing."

"Zing" has stuck with me. To me, "zing" sounds exhilirating. I liked it. Why feel "pain" when you can "zing"?

You don't have to be masochistic to enjoy getting after it. Just strive to be the King of Zing.

Shortcuts to Success

During a recent practice we were doing a series of short sprints. In the adjoining lane, a 17-year-old boy was swimming at speeds fairly close to what I was doing, but he was destroying me on the starts.

We both started at the same time, but I was dropping down into the water before pushing off. He was curling up to the starting blocks and jumping out over the water, as if he were doing a backstroke start with a one-half twist.

I liked watching him pull out all the stops in his quest for victory. His will to win was admirable. Thinking about it after practice however, it occurred to me that he had lost sight of his purpose.

Q: *What do you mean?*

A: I mean that the purpose of his training was to prepare to swim fast and to win at meets; and to enjoy that process. Winning in practice, though consistent with that purpose, is not necessarily the goal. In fact, such a practice goal can be counterproductive at times. Practice sessions should be devoted to *preparation* for meets.

His starts gave him a jump on everyone else in the pool, making him appear to be performing well. However, one never starts that way at meets. Everytime he did one of those starts he missed the opportunity to practice pushing-off and streamlining as he would after his turns in meets. Getting a jump on others only gave him the appearance of success, while the reality was that he was missing opportunities to build a solid foundation for success.

Q: *Let me understand. You're saying that we show off at the expense of training well; that we sometimes do things that only make it look like we are succeeding when we may not be succeeding at all?*

A: That's right. Ironically, we know we are kidding ourselves. For example, have you ever skipped laps in order to appear as if you are making an interval? Have you ever pulled on the lane lines during a kicking set in order to appear as if you are keeping up? Ever take a false start or leave early to make it look as if you were faster than you really were on a time trial or a timed series? How about taking less than the specified rest on a broken swim? These are like sucking in your gut in order to appear trim or only swimming fast during that part of practice when you think your coach is watching you.

If you feel the need to look impressive, it's easy to rely on shortcuts that will help give the appearance of success. No matter what your purpose or goals however, the appearance of success is a poor and short-lived substitute for the real thing.

Q: *That sounds so businesslike. Can't swimming just be for fun and recreation?*

A: Of course it can. But that doesn't mean that there are shortcuts to developing good swimming skills or speed. There aren't.

It's funny, nevertheless, how so many people who are in it for the fun and recreation go to great lengths to give the appearance of competitive success, often defeating their purpose in the process. No matter what your goals, it pays to act in a manner consistent with your purpose. If you are training to compete and win, you need to take full advantage of every opportunity to improve your skills, power and conditioning. You need to do all you can to get a jump on the competition. If you are swimming for fun and recreation, enjoyment must be paramount.

It doesn't do any good to train expressly to condition your body and to have fun, only to get discouraged about how you perform when compared with others. It is especially silly to do those one hand breaststroke and fly turns in order to appear faster than the swimmer in the next lane when you have no desire to compete. The shortcuts only make training easier and therefore less valuable for conditioning and less fun. The shortcuts may make you look good to someone failing to pay close attention; but it's tough to fool yourself, and tough to succeed, when you circumvent the path to success.

Championship Self-Talk

In swimming there is no substitute for natural talent, good technical skills, power, and conditioning. Given your present physical condition and immediate technical skills however, how well you swim is largely determined by your internal behavior: how you talk to yourself. What you say to yourself makes the critical difference in your performance.

Many people have insisted that the best athletic performances occur when an athlete's thoughts are still. Peak performance seems to come when the athlete is so involved in what he is doing that it just seems to flow.

In fact, the best performances do occur when a well-learned task of sufficiently short duration is performed without interference from thought. When a golfer has a much-practiced, smooth, technically-sound swing, he hits the ball best when he visualizes himself doing well what he wants to do, then does it without interference from thoughts.

There are times however, when appropriate thoughts are necessary for good performance. Among these are: when performing a task not yet over-learned and seemingly automatically performed, when changing strategy or technique, when adjusting to unexpected events, when skills for coping with expected but formidable obstacles (e.g. nervousness, or fatigue) are not well-ingrained enough to plug in automatically, when preparing for the task, and when the task requires more than a few milliseconds to complete.

In my work with some athletes, competitive golfers and tennis players, for instance, we work toward performing while so focused on the task that there is no awareness of their thought processes. Even in these sports however, where the actual task (hitting the ball) takes less than a second to perform, appropriate self-talk is vital. How well golfers and tennis players perform is largely dependent upon how they talk to themselves between shots.

In swimming, to date even the fastest swimmers in the world have required at least nineteen seconds to cover the shortest distance raced. In that much time, a swimmer will think. During the distance events, swimmers think a lot. The specific content of what you say to yourself prior to, during, and after a race, greatly impacts performance.

Do a good job of talking to yourself and you will be more likely to swim well. Talk trash to yourself and you likely will perform poorly. Fortunately, you can learn to control what you think about.

Self-instructions are one form of self-talk that can enhance performance. Self-instructional training can help you to become aware of your thoughts and to produce appropriate self-talk and adaptive behavior while minimizing the negative self-talk that interferes with good swims. Self-instructional skills can support your efforts to refine your technical skills and enable you to swim faster more consistently.

Before reading this article, you may not have paid much attention to what you said to yourself during a race. It is more likely that your thoughts were automatic and seemingly involuntary, like most habits. Your thoughts often may have taken the form of feelings and images, which you were probably less likely to identify. Even when your self-talk has been explicitly verbalized, you probably rarely attended to it. You can however, become aware of such thought processes and increase the likelihood that you will notice similar self-statements in the future.

In many ways the development of your self-talk while

swimming is similar to the automization of thought that accompanies the mastery of other motor skills such as driving a car. Those of you that are old enough to drive will remember that initially, when learning to drive a car, you had to instruct yourself during each step. You actually told yourself to put the car in neutral, turn the key, step on the accelerator, turn hand over hand, step on the brake pedal gently as if there was an egg beneath it and you didn't want to break it, and so on. Nevertheless, eventually the process becomes so well-learned that self-instructional verbalizations are no longer necessary. You seem to be able to drive without thinking about it. Half of the time, you probably don't even remember how you got where you were going.

Similarly, when learning new techniques or changing your form in swimming, you must explicitly verbalize the needed changes and cues. As these skills become learned, your self-instructions become shortened consisting only of cue words. Gradually, even the cue words seem to fade away, until finally, the process becomes totally void of all self-talk. Your movements become fluid. You only have to feel or imagine what you want to do in order to do it.

At first, having to instruct yourself temporarily may disrupt your performance. In the long run however, self-instructional methods will improve your swimming considerably.

Through self-instructional methods, you can identify, learn, practice and refine new and more appropriate internal behavior (thoughts and images) in order to increase the likelihood of peak performances. You can learn and utilize positive, task-relevant self-statements much more frequently. In addition, you can learn to identify self-statements that may interfere with performance and keep them to a minimum.

Irrelevant self-talk is distracting and can be detrimental to performance. Conversely, task-relevant self-talk is adaptive to the competitive situation.

Task-relevant self-statements may take a variety of forms. They may include:

1) **Questions About the Nature of the Task.** For example: "How do I want to take my race out?" "What would I do

well to think about during the race?" and "How can I approach this race?"

2) **Answers to These Questions.** For example: "Take it out loose and fast. Then negative split it." "Think about getting to the finish first." "Swim like Mark Spitz did the Munich Olympics."

3) **Guidance of Performance by Self-instructions.** These may include statements about what to do or what not to do. For example: "Drive into the turns." "Use your arms on the way out and drive your legs coming home." "Don't worry about your opponents. Swim your own race."

4) **Coping Self-statements** to deal with frustrations, anxieties, fatigue and discomfort. For example: "Relax." "Don't worry about what others think." "How can I use this anxiety to swim better?" "No one ever swims a perfect race. Don't let that turn get you. You can still be fast." "Okay, your arms feel it. You still can swim fast."

It has been demonstrated that individuals perform motor tasks better when in an elated as opposed to a depressed mood. Furthermore, it has been shown that self-verbalizations will influence mood level. By utilizing **mood-elevating self-statements** as "this is great", "I really enjoy this", "this is fun", or "I feel great", you can elevate your mood, thereby enhancing the likelood of improved performances. At the same time, you will increase your enjoyment of swimming.

Another category of helpful self-verbalizations is that of **self-reinforcing statements.** For example, thoughts like: "Great swim," "Way to go," "No wonder you had a good race, you kept your stroke," "That's the way to keep your elbows up," or "That's the way to think."

Self-reinforcing statements serve to maintain desired behaviors and increase the likelihood of these good performances occurring more frequently. Perhaps more importantly, swimming is much more enjoyable when you are rewarding yourself for a good performance, than it is when you are getting down on yourself for a poor performance. Make sure you notice the things you do well and acknowledge them to yourself.

Although it would be desirable to eliminate any and all negative, maladaptive internal behaviors, this would be an unrealistic goal. Even after you have become aware of how negative or distracting self-talk interferes with performance, you will continue to have these inappropriate thoughts occasionally. If you can learn to attend to these maladaptive thoughts and feelings when they occur and to use them as cues to signal you to plug in more functional self-statements; then you are well on your way to better, more enjoyable performances.

With practice and attention, you will recognize the negative feelings and self-verbalizations increasingly earlier. Then you can use these inappropriate thoughts as cues to plug in more useful self-talk. You won't eliminate all negative thinking, but you will minimize it this way and replace it with helpful self-talk when you do slip.

In describing his 1976 Olympic Championship swim, Brian Goodell provides us with some excellent examples of successful utilization of appropriate self-talk and examples of efficient coping with the dysfunctional thoughts that crept in even during this world record performance. As you well know, in a 1500 there is plenty of time to think. Hopefully a swimmer maximizes the frequency of functional self-talk and minimizes the frequency of self-verbalizations that interfere with performance. During the Olympic final, Brian repeatedly reminded himself about the nature of the task and directed his behavior subvocally: "I kept saying to myself, 'this is the Olympics; this is the final; get going!'"

He utilized self-instructions to cope with the discomfort and redirect his attention to the task at hand: "I kind of said, 'well, here's the pain, forget it and go.'" And when negative self-statements appeared, he was able to plug in more adaptive self-talk: "During the race the negative side of me was saying, 'you're too far behind; you can't catch them,'" "but the positive side was saying, 'get out, get going . . . let go of the cookie,' which means to get your head together and just get going."

Mike Bruner made use of some explicit self-instructions during his 1976 Olympic victory in the 200 fly: "I looked at the 150 turn and I didn't see anyone on my left, then I turned and I didn't see anyone on the right and I said, 'well, I got it. I've got to go for it.'"

Our divers also benefitted from appropriate utilization of these kinds of skills. Jenny Chandler, the 1976 Olympic Springboard Champion, recognized the importance of keeping her thoughts task-relevant and minimizing task-irrelevant internal behaviors. "I didn't look at the scoreboard," Chandler revealed. "If I watch the scores it makes me too nervous. I didn't know where anybody was the whole way. I try not to think about anything but the dive I'm doing."

The bronze medalist in that event, Cynthia McIngvale, was aware of her explicit utilization of self-instructional verbalizations on her all-important last dive. "I knew my last dive was one of my stronger dives and if I relaxed and went all out for it, I had nothing to lose," McIngvale said. "I just was thinking. 'Do what you've been doing in practice. Don't hold back. Go after it as strong as you can.'"

These Olympians demonstrated the usefulness of good, well-developed cognitive skills. It is possible for these skills to be acquired naturally or otherwise learned in some non-specific way; however, you may intentionally acquire these skills through explicit self-instructional training and conscientious practice.

As mentioned earlier, self-instructional statements initially may disrupt performance. Frequently, the visual image of the desired performance is preferable to explicit sub-vocal verbalizations. In the long run however, self-instructional skills will help you learn appropriate behaviors which will enhance performance. With practice, self-verbalizations eventually become short-circuited. You will become so concentrated and so focused on your performance that appropriate behaviors flow smoothly without interference from thoughts.

In order to swim well, technical skills are necessary: e.g. a good, efficient pull; a good, streamlined kick; a smooth, relaxed recovery; fast starts and quick turns. Once acquired, these skills may be sharpened through practice. Similarly you can learn championship self-talk. Then these internal skills likewise may be polished with practice.

Self-instructional skills will not plug in smoothly overnight. They take a lot of well-directed practice, as does the acquisition and refinement of any new skill. Tell yourself it will be worth it. Then tell yourself to work on your self-talk. Why talk trash to yourself? Championship performances come with championship self-talk.

EXAMPLES OF CHAMPIONSHIP SELF-TALK
~ ~ ~

TASK ORIENTED STATEMENTS

Pre-Race

What is it you have to do? [Then answer your question.]

Focus on your race plan.

Think about what to do, not about how you are doing.

Finish your stroke.

Be tough. Stay with it all the way.

Take it out fast.

Build going into your fourth turn.

Plan out your race. How do you want it to feel?
[Then answer your question.]

What do you need to remember about your stroke?
[Then answer your question.]

Keep your face relaxed.

Have fun.

During the Race

Be efficient.

Finish, push through.

Accelerate into the turns.

Relax your face.

Pick it up.

Stretch.

Drop your head fast after you breathe. [For fly.]

Legs up quickly. [For breaststroke.]

Head back and steady. [For backstroke.]

Bring it home, really kick.

POSITIVE MOOD INDUCING STATEMENTS

This is going to be fun.

This feels good.

You're doing great.

I feel strong.

REINFORCING SELF-STATEMENTS

You did it. Good job.

You're doing better. You're learning to talk to yourself
        more appropriately.

You hit your turns well.

I can really take pride in that effort.

So What?

Q: *I'd like to start swimming, but I'm embarrassed even to go out onto the deck. I'm in poor condition. I've been on a seafood diet (you know, whenever I see food, I eat it) and am twenty pounds overweight.*

A: So what if you are in poor condition and carrying twenty extra pounds? Are you a bad person because you've eaten too much and exercised too little? Are you that extra twenty pounds? Does it encompass your whole being?

Q: *Well, no. But with my spare tire it's going to be hard to get in shape.*

A: So what? Is swimming only going to be worthwhile if it's easy? Very little of what is fun, exciting and rewarding is easily attained. Anyway, getting in shape doesn't have to be that difficult. Start slowly. Take your time. Make it fun. Enjoy the process.

Q: *But what are people going to think when they see the Goodyear Blimp in a racing suit? Come to think of it, my*

Dunlap's Disease (you know, where my belly done-laps over my belt) will probably obscure everyone's view of my suit anyway.

A: So what? Who cares what others think? Maybe some of them *will* think you're disgustingly fat. Does that actually make you disgusting?

Q: *It's not only that. When I was in high school I was a real stud swimmer. Now, my grandmother can probably beat me. . . and she's been dead for seven years.*

A: So what? Did swimming fast in high school make you a better person than was everyone else then and than you are now? If others beat you, will that make you a lesser person?

Q: *Okay, maybe not. But I've always liked swimming with other people. I always enjoyed training with a team. I've been thinking of joining one, but what if I can't keep up?*

A: So what? Nothing catastrophic is going to happen. Maybe, at first, you'll need more rest or swim fewer laps than everyone else. If you're patient, you'll progress to whatever level you choose.

Besides, what's the worst that can happen? I guess it's possible that others may ridicule you, laugh at you, call you names, or throw you a life preserver. It's also highly unlikely that any of those things will occur. Even if they do, so what? Are you there for yourself or for their approval?

You can decide to feel bad about yourself based on what others say, on what you fantasize that others are thinking, or on some arbitrary standard of performance. But why do that?
You don't need to rate yourself on the basis of your weight, on your level of conditioning, on how fast you swim, or on anything else. In fact, it's best not to rate yourself at all. You may better decide to assess how worthwhile swimming is for you based on whether you are enjoying yourself, cleansing your body from the stresses of the day, burning calories, toning up and exercising your cardiopulmonary system.

Q: *I'm not sure I can do that. I'm too competitive. I'm not sure I can start swimming again without wanting to beat everyone in sight.*

A: So what? If you want to get involved competitively, go right ahead. There's nothing wrong with wanting to compete and to win. If it gets you engaged in your swimming, feeling alive and exhilirated, that's terrific.

Competitive swimming is wonderful. Competition only becomes a problem if you decide that you "have to" win, rather than deciding that you "want to " win. Why do you need to make feeling okay about yourself contingent upon who and how many people you beat swimming?

Q: *I've always felt like I've had to win in everything I do.*

A: So what? Just because that has always been your approach in the past, where is it written that you have to continue to need to win in order to feel okay about yourself? Why do you need to use your swimming to verify your worth now? So what if you race and don't win? Can't you enjoy the game and appreciate the good things you are doing for your body in the process of playing?

Q: *I guess I've never thought of it that way. I think I'm about ready to start swimming again. But what if I start feeling uncomfortable about my weight; or, if I slip back into my old abusive competitive ways after I've been swimming awhile?*

A: So what?

The Self-Image Fairy Tale

Once upon a time there were three little swimmers who dreamed of becoming champions. The three swimmers were a little porky, but they were trying to reduce their percentage of body fat.

The three little swimmers went out into the world of competitive swimming determined to build themselves into champions. On the road to success, they met a self-proclaimed "motivational expert" who told them about "self-image psychology" and all its magic. He explained to them that all of their actions, feelings, behavior, and even their swimming abilities, were always consistent with their "self-image." He told them that their "self-image" defined what they could and could not do.

And the "motivational expert" gave them hope. He told them that their "self-image" could be improved, and he described how, if they improved their "self-image," they would improve their ability. He suggested that if each of them saw himself as a winner, he would become one.

The "motivational expert" went on to suggest that the human nervous system could not tell the difference between actual experiences and experiences imagined vividly and in detail. He further explained that the brain and nervous system constitute an automatic guidance system, a goal-striving servo-mechanism which works for them as a success mechanism or a failure mechanism, depending upon how their visualized goals guided it. He recommended that, if they would visualize the desired results and not worry about the "means whereby," their computer-like, automatic, goal-striving servo-mechanism would get them to their goals.

The three little swimmers heard about the magic of self-image psychology and they were inspired. They all saw the importance of having some direction and not limiting themselves. So they set goals and worked to believe they could achieve them. They wanted so badly to build themselves into champions that they were eager to make use of any magic available.

The first little swimmer did not like to train. He saw training as work and he liked to play. He did want to be a winner. And he sure liked to daydream. So he spent a lot of time visualizing the results of the National Championships with himself as the winner. He clearly, in great detail, saw himself on the winner's platform. He religiously visualized these desired results, letting the "means whereby" take care of themselves. This suited the first little swimmer fine, because he didn't like to train.

The second little swimmer did not like training much better than the first little swimmer. He understood however, that part of feeling like a winner was acting like a winner.

The second little swimmer visualized success, but he also trained. The second little swimmer liked the idea of having an automatic, goal-striving servo-mechanism that would take care of the "means whereby," but he didn't want to take any chances. He thought he'd give it a little push and intentionally strive to train consistently well. He wanted *to be the best he could be*. So, having visualized success and trained pretty well, the second little swimmer swam confidently, knowing that the magic was working.

Now the third little swimmer was a sober little swimmer. He got inspired by the "motivational expert," but he didn't take the "motivational expert" too literally. The third little swimmer wasn't sure about this concept of "self-image." So he consulted a trained sports psychologist who explained that "self-image" was a convenient way of talking about the various thoughts and images that determine feelings and behavior. The sports psychologist further explained that self-image did not exist independently of those thoughts and images. The third little swimmer learned that it was more important to align his perspectives, assumptions, thoughts, images, and actions with his goals than to try to mold and shape his "self-image."

The sports psychologist suggested that the third little swimmer may not want to leave the "means whereby" to some automatic mechanism that may or may not exist. Furthermore, the sports psychologist suggested that the third little swimmer didn't need to think of training as a necessary evil for building a winner, but could rather view training as an exciting , rewarding and thoroughly engaging challenge, one that he may want to actively tackle on a daily basis.

So the third little swimmer set his goals, but he also devised an *action* plan for achieving them. The third little swimmer took responsibility for putting his action plan to work.

The third little swimmer learned not to limit his success by thinking of himself as someone who was good, but not great. He wasn't sure how imagining himself as a winner would make him one. But, the third little swimmer understood that he would have difficulty winning if he saw himself as a loser. He learned to open himself up to the possibility that he too could win. The sports psychologist asked the third little swimmer to consider that perhaps no one had the market on success, that perhaps no one was *supposed to* win. Maybe, he suggested, there were no "supposed to's" at all. Maybe victory was up for grabs. Maybe the third little swimmer, could dare to swim great.

So the third little swimmer trained intensely. Along with his physical training, he actively strove to prepare himself psychologically. He visualized himself *doing* what it takes to win. He learned that visualizations would help him to *cement* his action plan — to make it clearer and easier to do. He learned to groove-in good habits through this kind of mental rehearsal.

Occasionally, the third little swimmer visualized himself on the winner's stand. He didn't want to be afraid of winning. He learned to rehearse winning, thereby making victory a distinct and familiar possibility. He learned to remind himself of where he was going and to provide himself with some incentive for doing the things it takes to get there. But he learned not to think of himself as a winner. He learned it was better not to type-cast himself at all. Instead, he worked on his action plan, doing what he thought would be required to reach his goals. He strove to *do the best he could do.*

As the three little swimmers ventured further out into the world of competitive swimming, they found themselves coming up against many other hungry competitors. You could say they had entered a forest filled with hungry wolves eager to huff and puff and blow their dreams to pieces.

The first little swimmer had been making flimsy preparation. He knew he would win as long as he believed he was a winner. So he practiced thinking of himself as a winner and he believed in himself. He strove to mold a good self-image; but he neglected his training.

The first little swimmer also had little incentive to attack his races eagerly and vigorously. Since his brain could not tell the difference between an imagined experience and a real one, he had no need for goal-achievement or the satisfaction that accompanied it. He could gain the spoils of victory anytime he wanted to do so merely by imagining himself vividly and in great detail standing on the winner's stand.

You could say that the first little swimmer had used straw in his attempts to build himself into a champion. His hungry competitors huffed and puffed and easily blew his dreams to pieces.

The second little swimmer prepared much better. He built himself a foundation that was fairly strong. He actively told himself that he was a winner, visualized success and tried to act like a winner. He strove to be the best he could be. Often he trained well. Other times however, his automatic, goal-striving servo-mechanism didn't seem to take care of business. He wasted valuable opportunities.

The second little swimmer got stronger, faster, and had much success. Although he trained pretty well, he believed it was the magic of self-image psychology that got him there. He believed his good self-image was responsible for his success.

Even though the second little swimmer had success, it was tough to stay on top all of the time. The second little swimmer knew that when he didn't do as well as he would have liked to do, it was only a temporary setback. But when faced with defeat, he couldn't help but wonder why he wasn't succeeding if he had a good self-image. He feared that if he wasn't succeeding maybe he no longer had a good self-image. He began to have doubts. Maybe the magic was gone. Or worse yet, maybe he was being the best he could be and the best he could be just wasn't good enough.

Pretty soon the second little swimmer found himself occasionally afraid to commit himself and to go all out. What if he tried and didn't succeed? That could be proof that he had a poor self-image or that the best he could be was not good enough. So he entered competitions fearfully and protected his self-concept by competing half-heartedly. The foundation the second little swimmer had built had too many cracks in it — much like a house built of sticks. As a result, other hungry competitors huffed and puffed and blew the second little swimmer's dreams to pieces.

The third little swimmer had built himself a solid foundation. With intense training came improvement. With improvement an increased expectancy of success. This confidence made it easier to stick to his action plan. Action promoted more confidence — the third little swimmer kept winning.

When the third little swimmer fared less well than he would have liked to perform, he didn't think about self-image at all. He attributed success or failure to his preparation and his race performance — his actions. When he had a temporary setback, he revised his action plan. He looked for things he could do to keep himself on track and speed his motion toward his goals. It was as if he kept laying bricks and smoothing mortar in between. Thus, the third little swimmer strove to fill any gaps in his preparation.

The third little swimmer laid a solid foundation. When he raced, he boiled water. Other competitors came knocking at the door to victory like hungry wolves. But no matter how hard they huffed and puffed and puffed and huffed, they could not blow the third little swimmer's dreams to pieces. They only found themselves in boiling water with nothing to eat but the third little swimmer's waves. You could say they couldn't blow the third little swimmer's brick house in — not by the hair on their chinny-chin-chin.

The moral of the story is: There is magic in the action that makes for a good self-image, but not necessarily any action or magic in self-image psychology.

Or: It is not who or what you think you are that makes for success, but what you do.

What Might Have Been

As most of you know, in July, England's Sebastian Coe broke the world record for the mile run with a time of 3:48.95. An American, Steve Scott, finished second in a very strong field where 3:55.3 was good only for tenth place. Scott's time was 3:51.11 on the electronic timer, .01 of a second off Jim Ryun's 12-year-old American Record. The timers had Scott in 3:50.8. Even though Jim Ryun's record was hand-timed, Scott's electronic time was official. So, Ryun's record stands.

Steve Scott ran a very strong race. At the 400 meters he was second and fast. At the 800 meter point he was together with Steve Lacy in the lead — under world record pace. With 500 meters to go, Coe pulled even with Scott and then gradually moved away. Scott stayed with it. As *Sports Illustrated* reports: "Scott drove himself all out never letting the runners in back of him approach within eight yards. Then, inexplicably, he slowed before he crossed the line. 'I walked across, which cost me a lot,' he said later..." ("Walked" meaning he eased up and slowed down. In swimmers' terms: he glided into the finish.)

This all too familiar behavior cost him an American record. Ironically, it seemed so out of place in light of his goals for the race. *Sports Illustrated* reported that "for Scott . . . the appeal of the competition lay in its opportunity for non-Olympic abandon. 'I don't care who wins,' he said. 'I just want to run fast.'"

Maybe if he only cared about his place and not about his time, it would have been understandable. Then, when seeing that he no longer could win and no one could catch him for second, the race would have been over; "walking" in would not have been counterproductive to his goal. But he wanted to "run fast." As it turned out, this brief lapse of concentration (or perhaps, even a conscious decision to ease up and coast in) cost him badly.

In a sense, he made a choice to slow down. It may have been a conscious choice made at the moment. Or, at the very least, it was habit — developed by lots of conscious choices made in similar situations in the past.

Many of you have ended up regretting similar choices. You may remember going all out, trying to catch someone on the last lap. Then upon realizing that you were not going to catch him, you almost automatically eased up a little bit (or gave up completely), only to miss your best time by a tenth of a second.

Or maybe someone you usually beat got out ahead of you. Deciding that you must not have it, you let up. Only it turns out that you were out pretty fast. You could have finished much faster had you not let the other swimmer's breakthrough performance throw you off.

This past summer I watched a swimmer go after the leader on the last lap of a tough 400 meter freestyle. Although he swam a great last lap, with about three yards to go it became clear that he would not catch the leader. At that point, like Steve Scott, he "walked" into the finish, visibly letting up on the last two strokes. He could not have won. And he made cuts anyway. The few tenths of a second that he lost however, prevented him from breaking 4:00 for the first time. I know he would have liked to have those two strokes to do over.

Many times the decision to let up has nothing to do with a competitor. Rather, it comes as a resolution to the conflict between the attraction of your goals and the aversion to the discomfort derived from the pursuit of your goals. Often, there is a clearly defined choice point where you notice the discomfort, push through it, or give in to it.

What a difference making the right choice at that point can be. Satisfaction vs. disappointment, a victory vs. second place (or third or fourth or eighth), a best time vs. a mediocre swim, making cuts vs. staying home, or, as we've seen, an American record vs. a near miss all can hinge on a decision to stay with it and pick it up or to ease up.

At the critical moment of choice you must deal with the conflict. You may not like the discomfort or you may wish to escape the stress, which, of course, you can easily do by easing up, thereby slowing down. On the other hand, you have some goals for which you are striving. Their attainment hinges on maintaining or increasing the pressure.

Obviously you cannot ease up and stay with it or pick it up at the same time. Thus, the decision. A decision made on the balance of the factors involved. Though physically stressed, if you think your goals can be easily attained with continued effort, you are likely to stay with it. For example, locked in a close race with victory at hand, or with the knowledge that you are going fast and are on your way to making standards, a best time, a record or the like; you are less likely to give in to the discomfort. Even if the physical distress is intense, when your goal is in reach, you may push on. On the other hand, if you think you are unlikely to reach your goals, you are more likely to give in to the discomfort. The more intense the discomfort, the less likely your assessed chances of reaching your goals, and the less valued your goals; the more likely you are to give in. Whereas, the less the discomfort, the seemingly greater the chances of reaching your goals, and the greater the incentive for goal-attainment; the more likely you are to stay with it.

Unfortunately, when stretched to the limits of your physical tolerance, you don't always think clearly. Sometimes the discomfort seems so bad that your goals seem less important. It is as if you tell yourself, "Who cares? My goals aren't worth it." Sometimes you actually have such thoughts. More often, you lose it because you are focused on the discomfort and not on your goals. You just seem to forget that a fast swim is important to you.

Often you misinterpret the situation. As in the examples cited above, you may not think you can win; or you think you are swimming slowly anyway. This decreased expectancy of goal-attainment easily tips the scales toward giving in.

Sometimes giving in isn't *immediately* that big of a deal. You really would not have won anyway. Or you still would have been slow.

Similarly, sometimes staying with it does not pay off *in the short run*. You still don't reach your goals.

Nevertheless, *in the long run,* it matters. Every time you give in, you make it more likely that you will give in again the next time. Every time you decide to stay with it, you make it more likely that you will push through it again in the future. This is how habits are formed; habits which will determine those seemingly automatic reactions. Thus, often you find yourself easing up or staying with it without intentionally doing anything. It just seems to happen.

Though sometimes it may not matter, it is likely to catch up with you. Sooner or later it is going to matter very much. Even when it appears as if it isn't going to make any difference, it may very well. You may feel as though you are swimming slowly, give in, and just barely miss cuts. You may notice that your place has been determined and ease up, as did Steve Scott; only to just miss an important time. Or just imagine, in this Olympic year, noticing that you can't catch the swimmer ahead of you who has the last Olympic berth in her grasp; easing up and letting someone you didn't see touch you out for the runner-up spot; only to subsequently discover that one of the qualifiers got disqualified. Wouldn't that be a bummer!

The moments of decision often matter even when it seems likely that they will not. They almost always matter in terms of the habits you build. So, what can you do to better insure making the right choices?

Usually simple self-instructions are the most effective means of getting through the tough moments with the desired results. (See pp. 31–38.) By merely telling yourself to "stay with it," "pick it up," "beat that guy," "stretch it out," or the like, you effectively guide your performance.

Don't wait for these thoughts to appear spontaneously at the opportune moment. They may never come. Intentionally plug them in at the critical time.

One of the most effective things you can do is to remind yourself that you don't want to get caught at the short end of the stick when the race is over. You can be very explicit with yourself about that.

On the last lap of the 200 I.M. at the 1978 Long Course Masters Nationals, I knew another swimmer had the victory in hand. I didn't know where the rest of the field was, but I explicitly told myself that I didn't want to take any chances. I instructed myself to "put my head down and drive for the wall." I didn't breathe for the last ten to fifteen meters, drove for the wall, touched, and looked to the scoreboard to find that I had finished second, two hundredths of a second ahead of third place. Yes, I would have much preferred to win. But I sure wouldn't have wanted to finish third, a few hundredths out of second, because I hadn't gotten my hand on the finish pad.

Remind yourself at which end of close races you want to finish, which side of record times you want to butt up against. Simple signals or cue words will serve to remind you. For example, you could just think "time," thereby reminding yourself that those seconds, tenths and even hundredths are important to you. You could think "win," both reminding yourself that you care about a victory and instructing yourself to continuously, vigorously strive for it. "3 F" works for me. It reminds me that I want to have the first finger on the finish pad.

Of course practice helps. The more you practice thinking in a way that will help you push through these choice points and keep from carelessly letting up; the more often you will stay with the pressure seemingly automatically, out of habit. There will be times (probably many) when you will be glad that you did — or wish that you had. Just think how Steve Scott must feel when he thinks about what might have been.

Relaxed Speed

Relaxation is a tremendously powerful tool. It can be used to bolster confidence, manage anxiety, deal with the sensations that accompany effortful performance, enhance concentration, aid flexibility, increase speed and stamina, and promote a smooth, powerful stroke. Furthermore, relaxation is a pleasant experience and a skill that is easily acquired — especially by athletes.

Although relaxation is purposely and actively employed, it is passively induced. Relaxation occurs in the absence of tension. It requires no action. You merely let go of tension and allow yourself to relax.

Typically a state of relaxation (sometimes called "the relaxation response") is evoked by any of a variety of techniques, all of which direct the focus of your attention inward. You can induce relaxation, for example, by concentrating on relaxing each muscle group in turn as you move up through your body from your feet to your head (or down from head to toe), by focusing your breathing, by imaginally filling your body with a pleasant color, or by taking a trip in your head to a peaceful setting (i.e. the ever-present beach scene). The relaxation response, so induced, promotes a physical, emotional and psychological calm that best prepares you for stretching, combats pre-meet anxiety, paves the way for confidence, and conserves energy for the race. Frequently neglected however, are the massive benefits to performance gained through swimming relaxed.

Every movement is initiated and controlled by muscle contraction. For each movement you make, you can make an opposite movement. The muscles controlling movements opposite to one another are said to be antagonistic muscles. You get the most speed, power and fluidity of movement by relaxing muscles antagonistic to the prime movers.

Any tension in muscles you are not using impedes the functioning of the muscles that control the intended movement. In essence, any extraneous tension you produce pits one muscle against another, pulling in opposite directions and creating your own barrier to success.

Often this is what occurs when you try too hard. In an attempt to go as fast as you possibly can, you not only tense needed muscles, but inadvertently tense antagonistic muscles as well, thereby putting an added strain on your body. Instead of getting maximum power out of your muscles, you end up pitting one muscle against another. That can only slow you down, weaken the force you can produce, and tire you out. In fact, trying too hard can be so draining and inefficient that swimmers often report complete exhaustion after poor performances, while reporting that they feel as if they could have gone faster following their best swims.

Swimming relaxed conserves energy, thereby delaying fatigue. Muscular contraction uses energy. Excess tension wastes energy and hastens fatigue.

Relaxation is an important ingredient in producing speed in other ways as well. Swimming requires repetitive movements; you can't swim even one lap with but a single stroke. In order to repeat a movement, you first have to relax the muscle just contracted before it will be in position to be contracted again. Muscles contract rapidly. They relax less quickly. The more quickly and the more completely you can relax a muscle, the greater the speed and force with which you can use it.

Obviously you can't swim fast without muscular tension. You have to contract your muscles in order to move. But excess tension interferes with good performance. The key is to learn to swim fast relaxed.

Relaxed speed is a subtly employed skill. It requires isolating contraction in only the muscles you are using to go fast so that you maintain a generalized relaxation in the rest of your body. Skill at such differential relaxation comes with increased sensitivity to varying stages of relaxation and tension in individual muscle groups and with practice in relaxing unneeded muscles while appropriately tensing needed muscle groups. That is why I recommend that you employ a relaxation-tension contrasts procedure for relaxation training. Any of the numerous relaxation techniques can get you relaxed, but a relaxation-tension contrasts procedure sensitizes you to the contrasting feelings of varying amounts of tension in your muscles.

Instructions for relaxation training may be found in a wide variety of sources. The chapter on "Relaxation" in my book, *Championship Sports Psychology* contains instructions for numerous relaxation techniques including verbatim instructions for a relaxation-tension contrasts procedure. Wolpe and Lazarus' *Behavior Therapy Techniques* contains the verbatim instructions for the relaxation-tension contrasts procedure after which my procedure was modeled.

Relaxation tapes also are available from a wide range of sources. Almost any of these will serve you well.

Relaxation training should be coupled with practice swimming relaxed. Practice swimming fast while staying as relaxed as you can in the muscles not needed to swim. One place to get rid of excess tension is in your face. Though there is a tendency to grimace with effort, you can't possibly flap your cheeks fast enough to help you speed through the water.

As if excess tension wasn't enough of an impediment to speed, tension tends to spread. If you are tense in your face, the tension tends to spread to your neck. From your neck, tension tends to spread into your shoulders and upper arms. From there, it can directly interfere with performance.

Swimming fast relaxed doesn't mean easing-up or backing-off, relaxed speed requires sustained effort. The focus should be on relaxation-aided speed, not effortless performance.

You even may want to move away from the concept of "all-out efforts." It takes considerable effort to swim fast. There comes a point of diminishing returns however, where increased effort becomes "trying too hard," slows you down, and has a high cost in fatigue. Maximum speed doesn't come with maximum effort, it comes with optimal effort. Swim fast relaxed.

Making It

"What are you going to try to go?" one swimmer asked. "I'm going to try to make it," another answered.

I recently overheard that locker room conversation between two swimmers regarding an upcoming 1650. Then this past weekend, I heard a swimmer say she hoped she'd "make it" in reference to her upcoming 200m. butterfly.

How often have you heard other swimmers say that they were going to "try to finish" a 200 fly, 400 I.M., 1500m. or 1650yd. free? For that matter, how often have you expressed such lofty goals?

Swimmers don't really mean it when they say they just want to make it. They often just say things like that for the benefit of others. Nevertheless, when "making it" is verbalized as a goal for a swim, there usually is some underlying truth to the doubt inherent in the statement. That element of doubt, no matter how small, can deter good performance.

Our 200 flyer didn't have any reason to believe she wouldn't make it. Quite the contrary, she had gone three 200yd. butterfly repeats on the three minute interval, a straight 8000m. swim (alternating 50 fly, 50 free the whole way), and 16 times100m. butterfly repeats on the 1:25 interval earlier that week. She had made them all.

Here's a swimmer who had been able to make a 1:25 interval on 16 x 100s butterfly and she was worrying about making one 200m fly? Obviously she wasn't truly worried about finishing. She *knows* she can finish a 200 fly. So what was she thinking when she made a statement like that? I know what it means when I talk like that, and what often lies behind such talk, but I wanted to hear what it meant to her. So I asked her.

After a great deal of thought, she responded. For her, she said, part of it was the pain. She told me, "of course, I know I can finish a 200 fly. I had gone those 16 x 100s and that 8000. But there's always the thought that you may do it the wrong way, like take it out too fast and not be able to bring it back."

"And there is a little fear of failure in spite of the preparation. It may be a fear of looking bad, but more so, knowing how much it can hurt, and how long that second 100 can take when it hurts that bad. It's a combination of fear of embarrassment and the physical pain involved."

"It seems like pain wouldn't bother us. You hurt everyday, supposedly, if you're training hard. Going 15,000 a day and going hard sets, you should be used to it. But in a race, you try to go to maximum, and you're afraid of going too far. You see others take it out too fast and die. And you know you're not immune to it. You're just afraid you may overdo it going out. It's not really a fear of not finishing. I know I can finish. It's just that . . . you know how that last 50 feels when you go out too hard? The last 50 seems like an eternity. The whole 50, you're telling yourself how much it hurts and that doubles it. You're struggling to finish. Your arms are flailing and you can barely get them out of the water. It's a helpless hurt. When you're swimming strong, you are in control. But these times, it hurts and you can't control it. That's what I'm afraid of."

When she said that she hoped she'd "make it," she did so mainly for the benefit of those listening. "When I said that, I had been feeling pretty good, but no one really knew what I could do. I thought I would do better than most people thought." By verbalizing such a goal, she was trying to influence the expectations of others so that her performance would seem that much better.

She was also trying to lull her competitors into taking her

casually. "It's kind of a psych tactic. This way, they won't worry about me. Then maybe I can surprise them."

Then there was the peer pressure to verbalize such goals. "Everyone was saying that they didn't want to swim it. It was a way of going along with the gang."

Obviously she was not consciously aware of all this when she had casually said she hoped she'd "make it." Nevertheless, the subtle meanings that are implicit in what you say (to yourself and to others) affect your performance.

It is possible that some of you may verbalize "making it" goals purely for the benefit of others. Perhaps, when you do, you are trying to hide your competitive interests from some less competition-oriented friends. Or maybe you are trying to lull your competition into lackadaisical performances as was our 200 flyer. Even so, I think it is rare when such statements do not imply some fear and doubt. They certainly have the capacity to raise fear and doubt.

Even if such statements have no meaning other than their intended impact on others, they still warrant a closer look. Why would you want to hide your more competitive aspirations from your friends? Do you need to have the same goals as they have? Isn't it okay to go after superlative performances, giving it all you have? Saying you just want "to finish" may be a clue that deep down you have some doubts about your ability, or even your very right, to win.

If you are trying to con your competition into lowering their goals or suggesting to them that they too should fear not finishing, look more closely at where you are going. How far will you get? Such stategies are aimed at slowing the competition down. You may get past a few people this way, but not everyone. You are not going to be able to talk everyone into slowing down. Nor do you really want to do so. You need the challenges provided by good competition. To get to the top you must beat the best when they are at their best.

Often saying that you just "want to finish" is an attempt to excuse any possible poor performance. If you have this prior built-in excuse that all you were trying to do was "finish," you're safe. It is difficult to fail when you don't have to do well to succeed, all you have to do is finish. On the other hand, how likely are you to swim fast, if your goal is merely to finish?

Why excuse your performance before you swim? Are you that sure of failing? Maybe you're so afraid of failing that you need an excuse just in case? For that matter why would you need an excuse at all? The only reason to excuse a poor swim is if you believe that how fast you swim determines how good of a person you are. This, of course, is patent nonsense. Nevertheless, almost all pre-race anxiety is related to this very belief.

Like our 200 flyer, when you say you hope to "make it," you probably know you will finish. As she did, you are probably expressing some fear of the pain and some doubt that you will finish strong. You may not be consciously aware of the consequences of these negative suggestions, but you begin to worry. The fear increases the tension in your muscles. The increased tension makes you tire sooner and more easily. The tension increases your awareness of the discomfort that accompanies such an effort. Then you are less likely to finish strong.

Talking as if you just want to "make it" serves no good. It is not a very effective psych-out tactic. It invites doubt and fear in you and in your teammates. Worst of all, it obscures your true goals, deterring fast swims.

Go for the gold. Goals to "make it," just don't make it.

Happily Ever After

Q: *How do I stay motivated to swim regularly forever?*

A: Forever is a long time. The opportunities presented by a lifetime swimming program can be diversified and bountiful, the prospect tremendously exciting. The magnitude of the commitment however, can appear overwhelming, especially when you know that the responsibility for honoring that commitment is yours alone.

Former butterfly world record holder and Olympic champion Mike Bruner suggests, "you just have to learn to motivate yourself . . . 'cause eventually you're going to be on your own somewhere." For most of us Masters swimmers and adult recreational swimmers, "eventually" has arrived.

Despite good intentions, there will be times when you ask yourself, "why am I doing this?" You need to know why. Without purpose you lose interest. As Rod Strachan, 1976 Olympic 400 I.M. champion says, "people become apathetic because they have nothing to strive for. They have no goals."

Set some goals. Know where you are going and why you are making the trip. Identify some things you want to accomplish. Then when you ask yourself, "why am I doing this?" you'll have the answer.

Set lots of goals. Discover many different reasons for swimming. Then set goals consistent with each of these purposes. The more goals you set, the more engaging your swimming will be.

Q: *Okay. I can see the importance of goal setting, but what kind of goals should I set?*

A: Ones that work!

Long-term goals that state your general intention to involve yourself in a lifetime swimming program are a good place to start, but that's only a start. Good intentions for the long haul may not get you into the water on any given day.

Take your long-term goals and ask yourself, "what can I do to keep myself on track toward achieving these goals?" Decide what specific activities you best do, how you best do them, how much would be best to do and how often it would be best to do them in order to forge consistent progress toward fulfilling your long-term goals. Then set goals for each week, maybe even specifying what you want to accomplish each time you swim.

Your goals should be *action oriented*. Specify what it is you want *to do.*

Goals should be quantified and time-limited. Attaching numbers to clearly specified, time-limited activities will enable you to assess whether you have accomplished what you set out to do. For example, should you decide to swim at least four days this week, swimming at least 2,000 yards on two of those four days and at least 2,500 yards on the other two days, you won't have any difficulty assessing whether or not you accomplished your goals.

Doc Counsilman used specific, time-limited goals when he gave himself a year to prepare for his historic swim across the English Channel. He started off shooting for 40 to 50 miles per month the first couple of months, then increased his mileage goal every month, until he hit 160 miles in July. Doc achieved his goal for total mileage each month. By the last month, he had set additional goals: to swim non-stop for three hours six days per week, to kick one half mile continuously everyday, to swim more than 10,000 meters in three hours, and to take fewer than 50 strokes per 50 meters. He also set dates by which he wanted to accomplish a six-hour swim, then an eight-hour and finally a nine-hour swim.

Q: *I know I should swim regularly if I am to reach my goals, but sometimes I get in a rut. Then it seems like a drag to have to go to the pool. What should I do then?*

A: The first thing to do is to change those "shoulds" and "have to's" to "want to's." The main difference between work and play is how you view it. Wouldn't it be better to make swimming fun, than to perceive it as a chore?

Even if thinking that you "should" swim temporarily provides some motivation, such thinking takes its toll in the long run. Thinking you "have to" swim can make swimming a grind. If you think you "have to" do it, sooner or later you are going to generate a "who says I do?" and resist.

Anyway, if you think it out, you must conclude that, on balance, you do *want to* swim. Otherwise you would not have made a commitment to a lifetime swimming program in the first place. Acknowledging that you *want to* swim today is merely a matter of balancing any short-term conflicts with reminders of the value of your long-term goals.

Q: *Wait a minute. I'm not sure I have made a commitment to a lifetime swimming program or that I really want to. Could that be part of the problem?*

A: You bet. Specifying your intentions is one thing. Commiting yourself to action is another. Maintaining an ongoing program requires commitment.

That's not to say that you have to commit yourself to a hard-core, rigid training program or that you should view a commitment to swim as a "must-do" proposition. You don't. You may choose to commit yourself to an enjoyable, relaxed, easy-to-meet, flexible, personally-suited program of lifetime swimming.

Q: *It seems like it all comes back to making swimming fun. You know, I'm always glad that I swam. There are times however, when I don't feel like swimming. What do I do then?*

A: When you think you don't feel like swimming, remind yourself that you always feel good about having swum. Remind yourself that you will be glad that you did.

Remind yourself of the aspects of swimming that you enjoy. Then while you swim, focus on the pleasure and appreciate it.

I really enjoy the feel of using my body to swim. I enjoy the feel of the water. I find the water relaxing and revitalizing even when I'm just cruising. When I am pushing myself to the limit, swimming is totally engaging, challenging and exhilirating.

I find swimming immensely enjoyable. You may not enjoy it as much.

A lot of people ascribe to the philosophy that if it isn't fun, don't do it. I don't agree. There are lots of other good reasons for doing something even if it may not loom enjoyable. Swimming is one of those things that yields great benefits. I believe strongly however, that if you are going to do something, you may as well make it fun. If you are going to swim, make it fun.

You can make swimming fun. It is well worth the time and attention to do so.

Make swimming a social activity by finding a training partner. Make it a novel experience by trying new drills, new strokes, or even new places to swim. Or, take Mike Bruner's example. Introduce games into your training.

Mike used to work on "super walls" by trying to keep up with a teammate off the turn for as long as possible without taking a stroke. At the finish of repeats, he often picked out another swimmer, who was coming into the wall, and simulated a touchout situation, racing his teammate to the wall. You too can make a competitive contest or a cooperative game out of almost anything you do. Doing so adds to the enjoyment.

Take responsibility for making it fun. The more enjoyable you make your swimming, the easier it will be to maintain motivation for a lifetime program.

For All The Right Reasons

I swim for the health of it. I compete for the fun. I love to swim. For me competitive swimming is a passion. To me, swimming is integral to an exhilirating, healthy, fullfilling, and enjoyable lifestyle.

You may swim for health reasons, for weight control, for cosmetic benefit, for the social contact, for the joy of competition, or because it is just plain fun to power through the water. Whatever your reasons, take stock of them often; keep them close at hand. It is all too easy to get lost in the daily routine of your swimming program and to forget or distort the reason you swim.

The benefits to be derived from swimming are tremendously enriched by the challenge of competition. Competition challenges us to give, and therefore get, that much more. Easily forgotten however, is that much of the value of competitive swimming lies not in the results of the contest, but in the byproducts that derive from striving to meet the challenges inherent in the sport. Especially in our winning-isn't-everything-, it's-the-only-thing society, you can get caught up in the competition and make triumph too important. You easily can lose sight of why you compete.

Let's face it. We're not in it for the prize money. So what place does winning, or even improvement, hold?

Winning is important. It is clearly the goal of the game. The object of any swimming race is to see who can swim some particular stroke, some specified distance, the fastest. That's the game.

Much of the joy and beauty of swimming is enhanced by striving to win. It is, unless, you lose perspective and make victory more than it is. The contest determines who can swim that race the fastest under existing conditions at one particular moment in time; it is not a test of personal worth.

While winning is clearly the goal of any race, it need not be one's purpose for swimming. The *pursuit of victory* however, and certainly the *pursuit of excellence*, provides the means for fulfillment of most swimmers' reasons for participating in competitive swimming. Fitness, stamina, good muscle tone, weight control and many other sought-after benefits derive as byproducts of pursuing excellence in competitive swimming. These benefits are much more easily realized and more greatly derived when training and competing vigorously than when going through the motions of swimming. It makes good sense, therefore, to vigorously pursue excellence and victory in competitive swimming, even if you are in it merely to control your weight or to keep your body toned.

Unfortunately, too often we embrace the pursuit of excellence and victory for all the right reasons only to lose sight of our purpose as we get absorbed in the quest. Yes, the benefits are greater when we get after it. Intense training fosters physical fitness. There is great psychological pleasure in improvement and competency. The feelings of self-efficacy that arise with mastering your sport are rich and vast. And it feels nice to win and to set records. But what about those days when you stink up the pool, as we all inevitably do?

*

I recently had one of the SportsPsych swimmers express to me that she was getting down on herself because she felt as though she wasn't improving. She was feeling extremely frustrated over constantly bringing up the rear of the slow lane in practice. Of course, it wasn't true that she wasn't improving. She was

— rapidly. But then, most of us can relate to those feelings. Even if we are improving, it never seems as though we improve enough. On the other hand, she was correct about her status in the pool. Most everyone on the team was swimming faster than she. Was it necessary however, for her to get frustrated over her perceived lack of absolute or comparative success?

As I told her, she always has the option to upset herself if she so chooses. So too could she let her relative speed interfere with her enjoyment. But as I recalled, she didn't join our Masters team for the expressed purpose of winning the Olympics. She didn't expect to make a living off of the fame she expected to achieve from her swimming success. Nor was it a clear objective for her to swim a specified time or to swim faster than anyone in particular or everyone in general. She chose to join our competitive swim team for health, fitness and fun. She was training fairly hard and seemingly getting the physical benefits she sought. Her decision to get frustrated with her performance was the only thing that was interfering with her enjoyment. She would have preferred to have swum faster, but in her grand swimming scheme, it didn't matter at all.

She understood. For that matter, she knew it all along. She just needed to be reminded.

*

When your performance falls short of your goals and expectations, take note of all the benefits you derive from striving to excel. When you feel like "dead dog meat" in practice, don't you still burn calories, get toned, and build power? When everyone else is kicking your butt, don't you have a wonderful opportunity to work on your psychological skills? Heck, some of us even get to savor the experience of having a wife "clean our clock" in the power events. Is that a failed test of manhood, or grounds for divorce? What a great opportunity to discover that you aren't a lesser person just because someone, or everyone, can swim faster than you. Aren't there still challenges to absorb you and bring greater meaning to the day? For most of you, all you seek to gain by swimming is there to be had no matter how poorly you perform. It's there, that is, if you don't fill your head with garbage and an exaggerated importance of competitive success.

*

One of the wonderful things about our sport is that it provides such clear measures of performance. Most of us hardly do anything in practice without the pace clock sweeping along, timing the results. In meets our performance gets measured electronically to the one hundredth of a second. The clock doesn't lie. So we get immediate, accurate feedback as to the level of our performance. From these results we tend to set (and from time to time adjust) standards of self-performance from which we reward or punish ourselves. By making self-reward contingent upon our performances matching or exceeding our standards, we create self-inducements to persist in our efforts to reach our goals.

For the most part, this self-regulatory process provides the motivation leading to more vigorous, well-directed action and subsequent improvement. Sometimes however, our goals are too high, our level of commitment too low, or our actions misdirected. Some of us even find that working for a living gets in the way of our training! Then, when performance falls short, such self-regulatory systems can engender frustration, self-doubt, or even self-flagellation. Such times are great moments to remind yourself of the benefits you seek from swimming and to take note that you derive these benefits even when you're not causing yourself to be mistaken for Matt Biondi or Janet Evans.

The bottom line is that no matter how thrilling is victory, most of us choose to participate in Masters swimming for more basic and less fleeting rewards. To pursue victory is the game. To strive for faster swims: a personal game within the game. Health, fitness and a healthful lifestyle are the rewards. The benefits come from the quest, not the conquest. Remind yourself often. Keep your mission close to your heart.

No Excuses

Have you ever made an excuse for not swimming well? Did you ever make an excuse prior to your race, just in case you didn't swim well? Maybe you failed to commit yourself to superlative preparation; that way, you could always say you could have done better if you had truly committed yourself to your swimming. Did you ever refuse to accept a compliment because you knew you could have swum better? Did you ever make a show of your anger over a disappointing swim; perhaps you slapped the water in disgust or ripped off your goggles and threw them down? Have you ever been nervous before you swam?

These diverse behaviors all have a common source. They all stem from the very human tendency to judge yourself based upon how well you perform. We tend to measure our worth as a person based on what we do and how well we do it. For you as a swimmer, it is almost as though you are a good person, or at least a better person, if you swim well and a bad person, or somehow less worthy, if you swim poorly. If you stink up the pool, you tend to feel like a worthless piece of you-know-what. If you swim great, you may feel like hot you-know-what.

Do you know what an excuse is? An excuse is an attempt to justify your right to exist. An excuse makes claim that you are really an okay person, that the flaw lies not in you, but in some uncontrollable event or uncharacteristic mistake. An excuse says: "See that poor swim. That's not me. I'm better than that. I only swam poorly because: 'my goggles leaked.' "

Unless you were trying to protect some image of yourself, to justify your worth, why would you ever need to make an excuse? A poor performance would be merely that — a poor performance, and nothing more. It is only when you are trying to shelter your feelings of self-worth that you need to mask the measurement of performance with references to missed turns, recent illnesses, swimming through a meet, losing your goggles, or something you shouldn't have eaten.

Similarly, when you refuse to accept a compliment, instead discounting the quality of your performance; you are attempting to persuade others that you are a better swimmer than they may think and to elevate others' opinions of you as a person. (As if you somehow become a better swimmer and person if others think that you are.) Without such an underlying motive, why would you reply to a "Good swim!" with a "Not really. It wasn't good for me." or a "Nah! It stunk."? Otherwise you merely may say, "Thanks," acknowledging the compliment, and go on your way.

You don't have to be pleased with a swim in order to express thanks for a compliment, nor should you be impressed with your swim just because someone else is impressed. But neither is it necessary to reject someone's compliment and educate him as to how good you *really* are.

When you make a show of your anger and frustration after a poor swim, that public display works the same way. Such a display of emotion calls for everyone's attention and announces, "See that swim? It's not good *for me*. Would I be this angry if that was good for me? I'm better than that. I'm good. That swim was bad. I'm good."

That's not to say that you shouldn't be disappointed when you don't swim well. Disappointment is real and, most often, appropriate. Angry feelings may also be real. Whether or not anger is appropriate is another issue. To make a public show of your anger however, is but one more attempt to influence others' images of you as a way of protecting your self-image, one more useless act prompted by self-judgment.

Perhaps the most common and most problematic outgrowth of equating your self-worth or self-image with your swimming performance is pre-race anxiety. If your self-worth, your value to yourself, or your self-image is dependent upon how well you swim, then meets (or even time trials) can be scary. Instead of vying for a fast time, a medal, or championship honors, you are contesting your worth, your very right to exist. Such a threat can be tremendously disconcerting and debilitating. Instead of enthusiastically anticipating your swim, you end up nervously approaching (or avoiding) the race because you fear failure.

Though you may fail, failing doesn't make you a failure. You are not what you swim. Your performance doesn't define your person. Although the way you swim is measurable, you as a total person are not. How fast you swim may be an indication of how well you swim (measured against your goals, your best time, cut-offs, others' performances, or some other criterion), how efficiently you swam, how hard you tried, how well you prepared or something else, but it is not a measure of how good you are. The quality of your performance cannot define your identity. There is no accurate way of measuring your value or your worth as a person.

How could you accurately assess your worth? You could not possibly remember all the things you have ever done. Even if you could, how could you rate your acts in comparison to each other? What would you do, assign them relative weights, add them up, and, through some mathematical computation, come up with some measure of your worth or rating of yourself as a person or a swimmer? Such an assessment would be like adding bananas, apples and oranges. All you get is fruit salad. Your rating of your Self would be an overgeneralized and arbitrary conclusion.

It probably presents the most difficult and continuing psychological challenge in life, but you best learn to judge your performances without judging your Self. It makes sense to assess how you swam with an eye toward what you can do to improve future performance. It makes no sense, there is little utility, and it feels lousy to rate your Self. If you do, sooner or later, but inevitably, you will tend to feel inadequate and unworthy. If the cause of such self-judgments is your swimming, your swimming will suffer. You will swim more slowly and have less fun.

Accept yourself. You are not a good person. You are not a bad person. You're certainly not good or bad because of how well you swam. You are just a person, just a person who swims. Judge your swimming, not yourself.

Accept compliments. Make no excuses. Show no anger. Fear no failure. Just enjoy your swimming. Strive to go fast and win, but accept yourself whatever the results.

Swimming is a game. Play it hard. Play to win. But don't play games with your Self.

Caught In A Rut

When you first start swimming, progress comes quickly, easily, and in leaps and bounds. As you gain in skill, power, and conditioning, improvements come less often, in smaller increments and are harder earned

As a novice swimmer, development of even the most rudimentary skills increases speed dramatically. Similarly, the more you train, the better feel for the water you get and the more strength and stamina you build. With experience you learn pace and strategy. All of this yields an almost continual chain of progressively faster performances.

At first, it is easy for the effects of the quality of your training to be obscured in your steady progress. Particularly as a young age-grouper, you tend to go faster in almost every meet merely as a result of physical maturation. As you get bigger, stronger, and more coordinated; you swim faster.

There comes a time however, when you have acquired the basic skills, a pretty good feel for the water, a modicum of power and stamina, and your growth has slowed. Then, your performance may plateau.

An occasional lack of progress can be discouraging enough, but finding yourself in a plateau can seem devastating.

You may begin to wonder if you will ever go faster. Have you reached your potential? Are you over the hill before you ever made it to the top? Or, maybe the problem is all psychological?

Well, perhaps. I guess theoretically it could be possible for you to have reached your potential, but that is extremely doubtful. Human capacity is awesome. We tend merely to scratch at its surface. In any case, it is impossible to measure potential accurately. Nor is it useful to think that you've swum as fast as you can. Such a decision only serves to limit what you will attempt.

It is possible that you have set up some kind of psychological barrier to improvement. You may have limited your actions by failing to set goals, by setting goals that fail to challenge you, or by setting goals that seem so difficult that you feel hopeless about reaching such standards. Of course, if any of the above goal-setting problems pertain, then you may be able to get yourself out of your slump by setting goals that reflect achievements that you may attain readily through consistent, conscientious, well-directed action.

Most of the time however, the way to break through a plateau is to do something different. Most often that something different is training more, training more intensely, and/or training more efficiently.

If you have been going through the motions of practice, you will need to start being more consistently goal-oriented in your preparation. Of course, if you think you are already training well, a solution may not be as apparent. You may find yourself questioning the extent of your ability; maybe even thinking that you have reached your potential. Then, what do you do?

The first step is to see if you are judging your progress fairly. At the higher levels of performance smaller improvements are more meaningful. The faster you swim, the more difficult it may be to see your progress. You may be slicing only tenths of seconds where improvements used to come in whole seconds. It helps to remind yourself however, that even such small drops have significance in the world of competitive swimming, where national and international championships are often determined in tenths, and even hundredths, of a second.

That's not to say you can't make big drops. You can. So should you train to do so. If you are preparing to chip away at even a world record, you may get left behind. Somewhere along the way, someone is going to shatter the record. It may as well be you.

The point is not that you should be satisfied with small improvements, but that you should not be disillusioned with them either. Getting discouraged can only tend to hinder your progress; unless you can use the discouragement as a signal to get yourself doing something different, something that will help to turn it all around.

No matter where you stand on your climb up the ladder of performance excellence, when you seem to plateau, it's time to take some different action. If you are already training well, you may have to look for small refinements in technique and groove them into good habits. You may have to spend more time polishing your psychological skills. Or, no matter how well you are training now, you simply may have to put in more yardage at faster speeds.

A plateau is a sign that you are in a rut, not that you have reached your capabilities. To get out of the rut, you need to pave a new road to success.

Can Do

Q: *I lack confidence in my swimming. Is there anything I can do about it?*

A: Yes. You can take control and actually *create* confidence.
      Most of us think confidence is something we either have or don't have. It's not. Confidence is inferred from the manner in which we think, act and talk. Feelings of confidence are engendered by believing that you are capable of a specific action and predicting that you will be successful at it. Confidence is a result of things you do, not a quality you possess. Think you can, talk as if you can, and act as if you can and will; you'll be confident.

Q: *I've never thought of it that way. Where do I start?*

A: As you know, training leads to better performances. Confidence likewise begins with preparation. If you train well, you'll feel confident of swimming fast. The better you train, the more confident you'll feel.

Q: *No matter how well I train, it's hard to feel good about it. The amount of training it takes to do well seems overwhelming.*

The kids these days are doing so much more than I can ever conceive of doing myself. Knowing that, how can I feel confident?

A: Most of us Masters swimmers are acutely aware that we don't train as much as young swimmers do these days. We either don't have the time or we lack the inclination. That doesn't mean however, that you should feel ill-prepared for Masters competition.

It's also easy to fantasize that your competitors have trained better than you. Perhaps, they have. Most Masters swimmers however, probably haven't trained as well as you give them credit for doing. Meanwhile, you are probably better prepared than you think you are. In any case, it does little good to dwell on the inadequacies of your preparation or your perceived disadvantage to others, particularly to the kids. Don't do it. Instead, remind yourself of the things you *have* done to prepare. Intentionally filling your head with positive thoughts generates confidence and leaves little room for doubt.

Q: *That makes sense. I can see how focusing on what I did well to prepare will get me thinking confidently, but I want to feel confident. How can I do that?*

A: Recent psychological studies clearly demonstrate that thoughts trigger feelings. Think confident thoughts; the confident feelings will follow. Of course, the confident feelings may lag behind the confident thoughts. Change often takes time. You need to stay after it. Keep producing confident thoughts, even if they initially don't seem to produce the desired feelings. If you persist, the confident feelings will come.

Thinking, feeling and acting confidently interact in a self-sustaining cycle. Thinking confidently generates feelings of confidence; which, in turn, produce confident actions. Acting confidently reinforces confident thoughts, and so on.

You also may want to utilize a psychological technique sometimes called the "affect-bridge." Use your imagination to go back in time and relive an experience where you felt confident and swam well. Re-experience your past success. Then hold on to the feeling as you refocus on your present situation.

Q: *I often feel as though I'm capable of swimming well, but it's more of an "I'm-capable-of-doing-it — someday" or "maybe-I-can-, but-probably-not-now" kind of feeling. What do I do about that?*

A: Famed University of Texas football coach Darrell Royal once said, "Great potential ain't peed a drop yet." Thinking you're capable of swimming well isn't necessarily enough to generate confidence. You need to not only think that *you can*, but also that *you will*, that *you will now* and that *you will succeed.*

Q: *Won't I still have doubts come meet time?*

A: You may. No matter how you feel or what doubts may pop into your head, act with confidence. Act *as if* you have no doubts. Look confident. Stand or sit up straight and tall, yet comfortable and relaxed.

No matter how you feel inside, give a confident look. Appear as if you have it all under control and you know who's going to swim well — you are.

Don't engage in visual eavesdropping. You don't need to size up the competition. Let others check you out as you strut your stuff.

Don't express any doubts, even if you have them. If you generate confidence, others will feed you confidence. Do yourself a favor by letting others help you.

Attack your race with confidence. Swim as if you are confident, whether you are or not. It doesn't matter if it's only an act, a confident swim will more likely be a fast swim.

Such conviction is surely warranted. You may not have proof that you'll register a stunning performance the next time you climb up onto the blocks, but who knows? You definitely have no evidence that you won't swim fast.

Lesson From the Masters

Flipping through my files I came upon an article I wrote for SWIM SWIM magazine reporting on the 1981 Long Course Masters Nationals. Reading it again made me feel good inside. It wasn't what I wrote that made me feel good, but it is about what I wrote that warmed my heart. Some of the feeling came from the special memories generated from my personal experiences at the event. (How could I ever forget the moments shared talking with Edna Landon and watching her swim? This was one beautiful woman.) More of what I felt however, was the beauty of competitive swimming and how so much of the light illuminating that beauty shines through Masters swimming.

Masters swimming is wonderful. It gives us old people something to do. Ah, but do the young age groupers see all that Masters has to offer: the promise of swimming speeds of which were never dreamed until the dreamer found new context; the vast appreciation of the incredible health and cosmetic effects of training; the commonality of experience that reaches across race, gender, socioeconomic status and age, even leaping the boundaries otherwise known as generation gaps; the constant recharging of motivation, meaning and excitement brought to a pursuit by the magic of goal setting; and the

fostering of affection, support, encouragement, mutual admira-
tion and excellence engendered by competition in its purest,
healthiest, and most unspoiled form: competitive swimming?
These lessons are here, if we just listen to what Masters swim-
mers have to say.

What do a :23.89, a 1:50.56, a 2:12.83 and a 8:30.81
have in common? Let me put it another way. What do 26-year-
old Jim Montgomery, 88-year-old Nellie Brown, 33-year-old
Fred Schlicher and 77-year-old Edna Landon have in common?
An awful lot!

Where else but a Masters meet can men and women ages
twenty-five to ninety-something, from all walks of life, meet each
other for the first time and have so much to talk about? Where
else but a Masters meet can you find the makings for instant
comraderies, support, encouragement, and mutual admiration?
Masters Nationals is the pièce de résistance.

Despite the air traffic controller's strike, over nine hundred
contestants descended on C. T. Branin Natatorium in Canton,
Ohio for the Penn Mutual 1981 National Masters Long Course
Swimming Championships. They came for all sorts of reasons:

"People."
— Graham Johnston (50)

"Because I thought I had a crack at some National
Records." (She did.)
— Marsha Soucheray (40)

"To watch Gretchen [her sister] swim."
— Heidi Ernst (29)

"This is probably the only chance I have to win a
gold medal." (He won two.)
— Kevin Polansky (31)

"I appreciate being around such positive people."
— Jim Montgomery (25)

"It's a good chance to test out what I've accomplished during the summer."
— Edna Landon (77)

"To see old friends, to see people you swam with when you were 10 and under. I love it.
— Dot Wise (30)

"It gives women a great place to go look at men—all those little bitty bathing suits and those great bodies."
— Anonymous (35) by request

"Seeing all the good looking bodies of the young girls running around."
— Anonymous by request
(No, Kevin it wasn't you.)

The atmosphere was awesome. People enjoying each other, indiscriminately offering support, and appreciating one another. Susan Westnedge marveled at "such extraordinary displays of good health." Fifty-year-old Graham Johnston said, he "never ceases to be amazed and to respect the older people like the Lloyd Osbornes and the Jim Welch's."

Encouragement flowed as smoothly as Dot Wise's breaststroke and was far more plentiful. Rivals helped to shave the hard to reach back of opponents' legs. Pre-race "hugs and hugs" provided support. And, everyone cheered for each other. Swimmers lined the edge of the pool to watch Jim Montgomery's speed, to cheer Nellie Brown into the finish, and to thrill as Jaynie Hodgell and Heidi Ernst battled it out.

Comraderie, friendship, respect, admiration and encouragement permeated the atmosphere. But make no mistake about it. People were there to swim: to swim fast and to compete. And did they ever!

Jim Montgomery couldn't find the shortest routes around Canton (he kept getting lost between the dorm and the pool), but he found the fastest way to travel the length of the pool. Jim turned loose a record breaking :23.89 in the 50m. freestyle. The hard training he has been doing was apparent in his even more impressive :51.2 100m. and 1:53.78 200m. freestyles. Jim's comment was: "I know I can go faster." Watch out :49.37.

Sitting next to Len Silverstein as he casually caressed his legs with a razor, I asked him how he was swimming. "Pretty well," he said. "Are you winning some?" I asked. "I keep running into Manny," came the reply. "How in hell can I win when I keep running into Manny?!"

Lenny couldn't. At least not this time. Manny Sanguilly not only dominated the breaststroke events in the 45-49 age group, but following Saturday's events, he also gave a wonderful clinic on the breaststroke. Take note, Lenny. You may get him yet.

Meanwhile, I know how Lenny feels. There are a lot of tough swimmers to get past in my age group (the men's 30-34 age group was probably the strongest field in the meet), but even if I could have gotten past the others, the incomparable Fred Schlicher waits at the top. Fast Freddy handily won the six events he swam, setting a couple of National records in the process. His 2:12.83 200m. fly perhaps being the outstanding performance of the meet.

Marsha Soucheray won all six of her events in the 40-44 age group, as did Jane Katz (35-39), Helen Buss (45-49) and Dorothy Resseguie (60-64).

Edna Landon didn't have much competition in the 75-79 age group, but she was super. She took on the 50m., 100m. and 200m. breaststroke, the 100m. and 200m. butterfly and the 400m. I.M.

What a marvelous woman! I was somewhat reluctant to take on the job of reporting on the meet. Without doing so however, I probably wouldn't have taken advantage of the opportunity to meet Edna. I'm glad I did. Edna told me she was "not going to lose my zest for swimming." No wonder. She still has goals. "By the next meet I expect to have my fly a lot faster," she said. "Then, when I get that fly so it's speedy, I'm going to start on a flip turn."

Dot Wise looked pretty in and out of the water. Her breaststroke was not only unbeatable, but beautiful to watch. Her freestyle wasn't bad either as she cruised to new age group records in the 200m and 400m. freestyles. Echoing Jim Montgomery, Dot observed, "I can do better. I know I can swim faster."

Chris Ruppert nipped Dot Wise in the 200m. I.M. preventing Dot from a clean sweep of her events. Chris proved to be formidable competition for the rest of the ladies as well. She captured five gold medals, setting records in the 100m. and 200m. butterflies as well as in the 400m. I. M.

One of the most impressive series of swims at the meet had to belong to Graham Johnston. Graham not only won five events, finishing second in a sixth, but he destroyed the old records with each victorious swim. Graham sliced over seven seconds off of the 200m. I.M. and 200m. freestyle records, twenty seconds off of the 400m. freestyle record, over 25 seconds off of the 400m. IM record and over a minute and a half off of the old record in the 1500m. freestyle.

A group of vastly different people with similar interest and values getting together for some fun, recreation and healthfully, intense competition.

The competition renewed interest:

> "I want to train again."
> — Claudia Cronin (28)

And brightened a lot of lives:

> "We're having an awfully good time."
> — Edna Landon (77)

There's no generation gap here. Where else, but Masters Nationals?

Beyond The Words

"What's wrong with you?" "Can't you swim any better than that?" "That's got to be the poorest excuse for a swim I've ever seen." "If you think I'm going to waste my time and effort on you when you don't even try, you've got another think coming!" "Your problem is that you don't want it badly enough. You just don't care. Maybe you ought to stop kidding yourself and stop wasting everyone's time. Maybe you just ought to hang it up."

Sound familiar? How do you feel when someone, perhaps your coach or one of your parents, berates you like that? Remorseful ("I let everyone down.")? Inadequate and filled with doubts ("Maybe there is something wrong with me? I should've done better. I've had every opportunity, yet didn't come through. Maybe I don't have it. Or, maybe I really don't want it enough.")? Threatened ("Uh, oh. I'm going to pay for this.")? Angry ("This doesn't help. I don't deserve this. No one should treat me like this.")? Resentful ("Who are you to say that I don't care? What do you know? Let's see you do better?")? Worthless ("You're right. I can't do anything right.")?

Most of you have experienced getting chewed out like that. Probably you've felt some or all of the responses listed above.

Getting raked over the coals is not a pleasant experience. Most of the time, it doesn't even help much. You don't deserve it.

It would be better if others, especially those who care about you, didn't do it to you. But they do.

You can let it get to you. But you don't have to. You have other options.

While you may seem to just react, getting chewed out doesn't automatically make you feel remorseful, inadequate, threatened, angry, resentful, worthless, or any way at all. You get yourself feeling these ways by how you choose to react: how you interpret what is said and what you say to yourself about the experience.

When you fail to swim well, you don't need to be told. You know it. If you're like most swimmers, you're probably more disappointed than anyone else. You probably feel bad enough about a poor swim, you don't need someone else to get on your case about it. But they do.

Why upset yourself even more because someone came down hard on you? Why let someone get you down? Getting down doesn't feel good, nor does it help you swim faster. Of course, it is your choice.

You can respond to the words thrown at you. You can accept the literal message, feel bad, get down on yourself, think about how poorly you swam and how bad you are. You can sulk.

You can respond to the emotion you hear in the voice that is cutting you down. You can experience the anger and feel angry too. You can yell back. You can silently grit your teeth and bear the abuse, all the while cussing under your breath. Later, you can badmouth your coach or your parents behind their backs.

You can play the game, feigning humility and remorse: "I'm sorry coach. I don't know what was wrong. I'll do better. I promise."

You can defuse the anger with some tears. Crying often evokes sympathy.

Sarcasm is always an option: "You're right coach. There is something wrong with me. My character is defective. When I was swimming, I didn't care. I don't care now. I didn't try at all. I knew how much it meant to you for me to do well. So, I thought I'd stink up the pool, humiliate my coach, my parents and the team. I did all I could to impugn everyone's good reputation because I'm basically a malevolent, worthless piece of junk that not only has no right to swim, but shouldn't even be allowed to exist."

On the other hand, you don't have to respond to the words you hear when getting chewed out. You can look beyond the words, past the emotion, and to the intent that underlies the message being sent.

Whoever is chewing you out cares. He wants you to do better. He has confidence in you. He knows you can do better. He is trying, no matter how inappropriately, to motivate you. If he didn't care, why would he bother? If he didn't have confidence that you could do better, what use would raking you over the coals purport to serve?

Assume the caring and the confidence, ignore the words and tone, and respond to the useful part of the intent. Remember, your coach's and your parents' goals for you are similar to your own.

You could respond with something like: "I'm disappointed too. I really wanted to do well. I think I can. Perhaps, together, we can come up with some strategies that will help me swim the next race better. Do you have any ideas?" Or, you might suggest: "Maybe Monday we can sit down together and try to see where we fell short and what we can do to get prepared for future meets."

Or, perhaps, you just may look up at your coach, or your mom or dad, smile, let your eyes meet his or hers, and say, "thanks — thanks for caring — I appreciate it."

You Go Ahead. I'll Catch Up.

It was her first meet after what essentially had been a twelve-year layoff. Oh, she had swum some Masters meets and had swum half-heartedly a few years in College, but she had stopped swimming seriously after winning three gold medals as a sixteen-year-old in the Munich Olympics. Now, it was 1984 and Sandy Neilson was twenty eight.

It had begun a few months before. I love to train. She wanted to be with me. So she went to the pool and joined in on what otherwise would have been my solo training session. She was beautiful to watch. Not only good looking, but her freestyle stroke nearly flawless, with power and grace rarely seen. To watch her swim brought joy to my eyes.

She was still fast. I already knew that from watching her in Masters competition. But here as I watched the great technique, the power and speed which she generated off of so very little training and no weights, my mind boggled with fantasies of what she could accomplish with weight training and a mere modicum of serious swimming, let alone if she really got after it. So I casually observed to her that I thought she could break the world record in the 100 meter freestyle. As she listened to me, I caught the gleem in her eyes.

Having competed in Masters competition had prevented her from competing as an amateur. She wasn't a professional swimmer, but had competed in Masters competitions where professionals were allowed to swim, thus she was "contaminated." In 1984, too late for Sandy to qualify for the Olympic Trials, the rule was changed. Now she was free to compete internationally, even though she had swum in Masters meets.

The door open, it was time to step in. We searched for a Senior Meet in which Sandy could attempt to qualify for the 1984 U. S. Swimming Long Course National Championships. We found one in Clovis, California. Unfortunately, it was the same weekend as the opening ceremonies for the 1984 Los Angeles Olympics. I say, "unfortunately" because Peter Ueberroth, Director of the Los Angeles Olympic Organizing Committee, had asked Sandy to join five other Olympic Champions in carrying out the Olympic flag in the opening ceremonies.

It was a tough decision, Peter Ueberroth's offer was quite an honor and, as it turned out, the six Olympians carrying out the flag received a tremendous amount of publicity. But Clovis would be her only opportunity to make cuts for Nationals. If she was going to commit herself to making the 1988 Olympic team, it seemed as though the time was now.

Not that cuts would be easy. In 1984, the qualifying standard for the 100 meter freestyle was the same time, to the hundredth of a second, as was Sandy's winning time in the 100 meter freestyle in the 1972 Olympics; and she was twelve years removed from that swim.

It didn't seem as if anyone noticed her presence at first, but slowly the coaches started to notice that Sandy was entered. Heck, a lot of the coaches had swum with her or knew of her from the early 1970's.

As I write this, an older entry may not seem especially bold. Sandy has made quite a splash in the aquatic world. Largely as a result of her paving the way, it isn't that unusual now for older swimmers to compete. Many swimmers are staying with it longer. Many have made comebacks. But at the time, it was unheard of for a 28-year-old woman to be competing other than in Masters meets.

We had just sent in Sandy's entry without any fanfare. Later, media coverage would get big and would be important for some of the things she wanted to, and would, accomplish. For now, she just wanted to swim and to qualify for nationals.

Sandy swam the 50 meter freestyle on the first day of the Clovis meet. When she swam the prelims, she was fairly inconspicuous. Her first swim after all these years was a little tentative. She swam next to swimmers who were half her age and she felt somewhat out of place. She was nervous. And why not, soon all eyes would be on her. Moreover, she had passed on a once-in-a-lifetime opportunity in order to gamble on cuts. After she swam, she would tell me that when she got up on the blocks her heart was "racing like a little bunny rabbit's."

Her time in the fifty easily qualified her for finals (she had the second fastest time), but she had missed cuts by a mere two hundredths of a second. She'd have to get it at night.

We really wanted the 50 cut. Not having as much time to prepare, we felt that she had a better shot at the 50 than at the 100 (though we wanted to think she could make the 100, even considering that she would have to swim a lifetime best time, faster than she did when she won the Olympics twelve years earlier).

That evening the pool deck was abuzz with chatter about Sandy: "Did you see who's swimming the 50?" "Check this out, she's 28," and so on. Coaches were telling their swimmers to watch this woman swim, some wanting them to catch the novelty of an old lady competing, others because they knew the beauty and efficiency of her stroke, and still others grabbing at the chance for their swimmers to glimpse an Olympian. The sides of the pool had been relatively empty for the earlier events. As the time approached for the women's 50 meter freestyle final however, the deck was lined with swimmers and coaches watching, and pointing, in anticipation of Sandy's swim.

The horn went off. Sandy was quick off the blocks. She entered the water respectably on her dive, but was slow breaking out. Then she took the weirdest first two strokes. (Maybe they didn't look weird to others, but I knew how she swims and this wasn't she.)

It turns out that Sandy, who wears her contact lenses when she swims, lost the seal on her goggles when she dived in. Her goggles filled with water. She had a choice. She could swim with her eyes closed until she smashed into the wall; she could open her eyes, kiss her contacts goodbye (contacts for which Mom and Dad no longer paid) and grope for the wall; or, she could do what she did. She stopped, treaded water and fixed her goggles. Not your everyday manner of swimming the finals of a 50 in a Senior Meet. She not only got to put on this unusual performance, but she got to do it with the spotlight and all eyes fixed on her.

By the time her goggles were adjusted, the field was a body length ahead and she was dead in the water. Then she took off like a bat-out-of-hell. I've never seen a woman swim that fast. The fourteen-year-old who won the race made cuts for Nationals. Sandy almost caught her. Another five yards and she would have had her. Sandy went 27.9 for a 50m. freestyle that included a stop to adjust her goggles. It's amazing the power one can find in trying to bust through an embarrassing situation.

It was easy to imagine how she felt, pulling that stunt with everyone watching. I rushed from my position with the other coaches on the side of the pool and made my way toward the finish end of the pool to get to Sandy. She had climbed out and was hurriedly slinking away toward the locker room when I caught up with her. I put my arm around her, met her tearful gaze with my eyes, and cracked up. I laughed and laughed until she laughed too. Heck, it was just a swimming race. And it was funny! Then, I asked her what happened. I told her how funny she looked stopping to fix her goggles and I told her how unbelievably fast she was thereafter.

Hey — sometimes you miss. Sometimes you get it. But it's always just a race. And except when there's prize money on the line, it's all just for fun. It's fun to race, even when you give everyone else a head start. So Sandy and I made our way to the clerk of course to enter that night's time trials.

A half hour later, Sandy made cuts in the 50. The next day, she swam the 100 faster than she did in the Olympics, making standards in that too. The rest is history in the making.

When Sandy won the Olympics her time seemed fast. I

guess it was. No one had ever gone faster. But twelve years later, her 1972 winning time didn't look that fast. A woman had to swim that fast merely to qualify for Senior Nationals. So Sandy went faster — twelve years later, in her first race back. In 1988, she went even faster than that unshaved and untapered. She is yet to go as fast as she will go; and as of this writing, she is 35-years-old.

Fast is what you think is fast. You can swim so much faster than you ever before thought was possible. You just need to decide that what you previously thought was fast is not that fast after all; and it is not fast for you. Then, you need to train knowing that is true.

Open yourself up to the idea that you can swim so much faster than you ever before thought was possible. There are still new speeds to be attained. Don't wait for others to show you how. You don't need to give them a head start. Pave the way.

Training Alone

Q: *I regularly swim alone. I'd like to continue my training, but sometimes it's tough to get going on my own. It isn't as much fun as training with a team. What can I do?*

A: Novelty is one thing that makes swimming with a team more enjoyable. Coaches put a lot of time and attention into developing varied practice routines. When swimming alone, too many swimmers put in their yardage in the same fashion everyday. How many people, who regularly swim 2,000 yards, for example, do something like: 1,000 swim, 500 pull, 500 kick? The same thing everytime.

Take the time to write out an interesting practice prior to heading for the pool. If you don't feel creative or don't want to take the time, pull one out of a book. At least get out of the rut and change the order — maybe kicking first occasionally.

Some swimmers trade practice ideas. (Which reminds me. Kevin Polansky wrote to me asking to trade practices. I've yet to write back — Kevin: Yesterday I went an 800 mixer warm-up, 2[P 500, P 5 x 100 x 1:15], S 8 X 150 X 2:15 [middle 50 stroke, I.M. order, average 1:45], 200 warm down.)*

The more you can do to introduce some novelty into your swimming routine, the less likely you are to get bored.

Swim in a different lane than you usually do. Or, start from the other end of the pool. Better yet, if you're not doing a timed swim, start at one end and snake the pool, moving to a different lane with every lap. Who knows? You may even meet some nice people this way.

Q: *I think that introducing variety would help to keep it interesting. I'll do that. But what about training hard? It seems so much tougher to get going when I'm swimming alone.*

A: It *is* tougher. When swimming alone, it's easier to get lost in questioning your motives. It's more difficult to find the incentive to train hard. When a coach gives you a tough set and sends you off, you are not as likely to spend a lot of time trying to decide whether or not you want to do it. Likewise, swimming with a team provides built-in competition for every practice swim, effectively diverting your attention away from the uncomfortable rigors of physical effort.

Herein lies another reason for writing practices out in advance. If you do, each item takes on the "this is next" flavor of a well-structured practice. Then you don't have to find sufficient justification for everything you do. Each drill is merely what is next.

Though you may not have the ready-made competition inherent in a team practice, you can build competition into your solitary practices. Set some goals. Then, swim against the clock. Pick out someone else in the pool and go after them. No matter that he is not swimming the same set as you, try to lap him; try to stay within a lap of him; or use him in whatever way presents a challenging goal.

---

* Editor's note. Keith swam 800 yards of various strokes to warm up, followed by 500 yards of straight pulling. He then pulled 100 yards of freestyle five times leaving every minute and 15 seconds regardless of the time it took him to pull each 100. He then did the 500 and five 100 pulls a second time. After that he swam 150 yards eight times leaving every two minutes and 15 seconds. This last "set" was juiced up by the inclusion of 50 yards of each stroke (butterfly, backstroke, breastroke and freestyle) on the middle 50 of the 150-yard swim (the first and last 50 of which was done freestyle). (I.M. is short for individual medley, an event in which all four strokes are swum in succession in the order just described.) Then he swam an easy 200 yards to warm down.

Tell someone, anyone, what pace you are going to hold. He may not care or even watch, but a verbal commitment, even to an unknown lifeguard, can be a spur to greater effort. (Who cares if he thinks you are weird or presumptuous? Tell him your psychologist suggested that you openly share your goal times.)

If you're feeling lazy, hop out of the water and sprint a 25 from a dive. The momentum from the dive can help you get past the sluggishness. Often the most difficult barrier to getting a good training session is getting past the timidity toward going hard. Once you have gotten past your inertia and gone one hard swim, it is usually easy to push yourself over and over again.

Use your imagination. Imagery can transform a challenging practice swim into a tight race for the national championship. A swim focusing on stroke technique can become a demonstration of proper technique before a well-attended clinic.

Use the "as if" method. Swim *as if* you are someone else. Approach a set of repeats *as if* you are Mike Bruner (holder of the Olympic 200 meter butterfly record) swimming the same set. Swim a descending set of I.M.s *as if* you are Tracy Caulkins. Swim *as if* you are enjoying yourself and *as if* you are eagerly seeking out more and tougher challenges. Swim *as if* you are still young, energetic and highly motivated to excel.

You may want to keep records of your practice times and use them as a basis for setting goals for the next time you do the same set. Select a variety of sets to record so that you won't have to repeat any one set too often. Then set a goal to go better than your average for all the times you've done in a given set.

1968 Olympian Pete Williams, who now trains on his own, says that he commits himself to four or five main series that he rotates throughout the week. Then he compares his performances from one week to another.

Pete also recommends using fins occasionally. "You really get up on the water and get the feeling of speed while getting a good workout," he says. He likes the idea of "record days," when you put on the fins and go after some records, whether National records for your age group or personal bests. And, of course, fins allow you to go more yardage (if you're into going more yardage) in a shorter time, especially when kicking.

Swimming alone can produce just as much enjoyment and conditioning as training with a team, though training alone may present a more formidable challenge. The responsibility for making training interesting and keeping yourself going is yours alone. You don't get any help. But all it takes is a little planning and some consistent creative action. As Austin masters swimmer Bill Jorn says, "The satisfaction from a good workout on your own, from giving yourself some tough goals and tough intervals and making them, makes you feel like a million bucks — because you did it all yourself."

Perceived Disadvantage

You are swimming stroke for stroke with the swimmer in the next lane in a 1650. You're struggling to maintain the pace. You're not sure how long you can keep it up. Your competitor however, shows no signs of weakening. As you look at him underwater, he seems to be going strong. His arms are maintaining a steady rhythm. Like the motor-driven, paddle-wheel blades on a riverboat, they keep churning away. Each stroke looks like the one before, every one powerful and efficient. His kick swells up a steady stream of white water. There's not a hint of slowing down.

Sometimes the contrast between how you think you are faring and how others seem to be doing can be very discouraging. Such a perception can make it hard to go on. You seem to have it so much worse than they do. It's almost as if other people were ahead of you in line when the ingredients for success were being passed out.

Sometimes you find yourself acting as if you have some basic disadvantage or you perceive yourself to be inferior to others. It may seem like you can't train as hard or swim as fast as others because you are lacking in some important quality or trait. You may wonder if you have that "burning desire" or the "mental toughness" it takes to win. If you don't, how can you compete?

This perceived disadvantage usually emerges in some mistakes in thinking about how you stack up against other swimmers in your experience of the challenges inherent in competitive swimming or in your ability to cope with those challenges. You may mistakenly believe that at least some other swimmers don't get tired, don't feel the discomfort accompanying effortful performance, don't get distracted or don't get bored. You may incorrectly conclude that some other swimmers have access to some ways (to which you are not privy) of staying on track, making practices more fun or of making their effortful swims less distressing than yours. Or, though others feel discomfort, it may seem as though the nature of their discomfort is somehow qualitatively different from yours. In each of these cases, you feel disadvantaged because others' ability to train hard, and to swim fast, seems to be less impaired by swimming's obstacles than is yours. They seem uneffected; or, at least, seem to find it easier than you to swim well in spite of the difficulties.

These misconceptions come easily. For one thing, you have had experiences where you were acutely aware of the discomfort when swimming, but it didn't seem to matter. It may have even felt good to go fast in spite of the discomfort. Similarly, there have been times when you found it easy to stay focused and to make even the most seemingly monotonous practices fun. You really got into them and found them exhilirating. Unfortunately, you don't experience your swims this way all the time. It may seem however, as if others always do (or, at least, more often than you do — and certainly right now.). Therefore, you appear to be at a disadvantage.

Another factor contributing to some perceived disadvantage is that you get deceiving information. There is a big difference between the experience of swimming and that of watching someone else swim. It looks a lot easier than it feels. While it may look as though your competitor is going strong, you have no way of knowing how he feels. You simply cannot feel another swimmer's discomfort. You have no access to others' internal experience. You can't "hear" their disinterest, their doubts, or their worries about their ability to handle the discomfort, to maintain their pace or to have anything left for a strong finish. Neither can you see how good and strong you look. Unfortunately, much of what you don't see, feel, or hear doesn't seem to exist.

No matter how reasonably acquired, this perceived disadvantage is clearly not useful. It never does you any good to think this way. Instead, it is helpful, in these situations, to remind yourself that you cannot feel or otherwise know what goes on inside other swimmers, but that, more than likely, they experience the struggle much the same as you. You are not disadvantaged at all.

You may even want to talk with others about the nature of their swimming experiences. This can help confirm that other swimmers' experiences are very similar to yours. A group talk about these issues can be particularly revealing. Of course, it helps to discuss these issues with swimmers whom you trust to be open and honest about their experiences. Some swimmers may not be willing to share their true experiences with you. They may recognize the competitive advantage gained by never appearing to get tired, by seeming to be uneffected by the stress, and by looking as though they always enjoy practice and competition.

Some of the better swimmers may honestly discount the challenges, reporting something like, "It's not that bad." And it may not be bad for them, not because they are inherently advantaged, but because they have learned to cope by relaxing and not worrying; strategies you too can easily acquire.

Others may be handling the stumbling blocks better. They may be more powerful, in better shape, swimming more efficiently, or they may be employing better psychological skills; but these are advantages you can eliminate. You can gain power and conditioning through intense training, you can learn to swim more efficiently and you can acquire good psychological skills. This is not a question of inherent advantage or disadvantage. It is a question of preparation.

When you are locked in a head-to-head battle with a competitor, it is likely that the race is close because your respective levels of preparedness are similar. Then, it remains to be seen what you will do with the common obstacles you combat while battling each other. Will you tell yourself that you don't have it and that your competition is better than you. Or will you decide that you are on equal footing, that victory is up for grabs, and to go for it. The choice is yours.

Resourceful

Motivation for training with the consistent intensity and precision likely to get you to the top is partly determined by the meaningfulness of your training. You must believe that what you do in practice, and how well you do it, directly affects how well you will swim in meets.

Most of you probably believe that training is important. You probably have a general belief that if you train well, you will do better in meets. There must however, be some specificity of beliefs. You must understand that each thing you do in practice is an important ingredient in the formula for success. That's not always easy to see.

Training for competitive swimming defines your lifestyle. Practice tends to be where you go and what you do at that time of the day. The routine sometimes overshadows the purpose of practice. It becomes easy to go through the motions. It's easy to lose sight of the importance of any given swim, drill or an entire practice session. Each one is only one of so many.

A better understanding of what training is all about (what it is intended to accomplish, how that is best done, and what are the likely effect of various training routines and behaviors) makes practice more meaningful and generates greater motivation. That increased understanding comes through education.

It's too bad schools don't offer courses in competitive swimming. Wouldn't it be wonderful for math teachers to focus on teaching students to read a pace clock, calculate splits, and figure paces and intervals? Science classes could consist of biomechanics, exercise physiology, nutrition, and kinesiology; all directed at enhancing competitive swimming performance with great specificity. Of course, everyone would want to take swimming psychology. Unfortunately, such curriculum is not available in most school systems.

There are however, great resources for attaining your swimming education, the most obvious and readily available being your coach. Most of you train within a program that is structured in such a way that your coach has the responsibility for planning and orchestrating training. This allows you to avail yourself of your coach's background, experience and expertise.

Most successful coaches put a great deal of care into designing their training regimens. They draw upon their knowledge of exercise physiology, biomechanics, kinesiology, sports psychology, and the stategies and philosophies of competitive swimming.

Despite all this planning, it used to be that coaches would tell their athletes what to do, then expect that their athletes do it without question. No need was seen for athletes to understand the principles guiding their training, as long as they followed the program. Fortunately, more and more coaches are recognizing the importance of understanding. Coaches are coming to see that athletes are more motivated to train when training seems more meaningful. As a result, increasingly more coaches are educating their swimmers.

Hopefully, your coach has chosen this route. Nevertheless, you are ultimately responsible for your training and for getting yourself motivated to train. Help yourself get motivated to train better more consistently by taking it upon yourself to learn and understand the purpose and underlying principles behind your training.

Take responsibility for understanding what it is that you are trying to accomplish and how that is done best. Seek out that understanding. Make good use of the resident expert: your coach. If your coach doesn't volunteer a lot of information, don't be afraid to ask questions.

Ask questions. Don't question. The way you ask is important. Putting a question to your coach about training is significantly different than questioning the training program. The former is an inquisitive request designed to aid your understanding. The latter comes off as a challenge, demanding that your coach justify all or part of the program.

Coaches need not justify their programs to their swimmers; nor would most coaches be inclined to do so. They only need sell their service, hopefully through quality performance. Most coaches however, would be willing to aid understanding and motivation. In fact, I suspect they would be eager to do so.

Timing is important too. Your coach probably will not have the time nor the inclination to adequately explain the advantages of a particular drill in between a "ready" and a "go." Most coaches however, would be willing to take some other time to do so. Ask your coach when would be the most convenient time for questions.

Remember, you and your coach are engaged in a cooperative effort to get you swimming faster and to enrich your competitive swimming experience (personally as well as athletically). Education is a key component in that process and a major source of the positive expectancy that increases the motivation to train.

Written matter is another tremendous source of information. There are a number of good books out on the science of swimming, training, stroke mechanics, flexibility, weight training, exercise physiology, and sports psychology. (I even know someone who has written some good books on sports psychology for swimmers.) Swimming periodicals offer articles that can aid your understanding of the critical issues involved in training for competitive swimming. Read about your sport. Superlative meet preparation is fertilized with knowledge.

Clinics, films, and tapes (audio and video) can be other sources of helpful information. So too can be the exchange of ideas and information with your fellow swimmers.

Utilize all the resources available to you. Take the time, and put forth the effort, to learn about your sport. The more you know about what you are asked to do in practice and how it will aid you in your quest for excellence, the more eagerly you are likely to attack practice and the more well-directed and, as a result, productive, your efforts likely will be. In swimming, as in most everything else, education is part of the combination that unlocks the vault which harbors success.

Nothing To Lose

Q: *I've had a pretty good rivalry going with a fellow Masters swimmer. We've been trading victories back and forth in a series of close races. Then in our most recent race, she blew me out of the water. How do I handle such a resounding defeat?*

A: Dwelling on defeat serves no purpose. It only needlessly upsets you.

Instead, identify those things you did, failed to do or might have done better that directly led to your getting beat. Then let that assessment help you develop future goals. It's helpful to chart out a future course of action. It's never beneficial to replay constantly the *product* of past unsuccessful actions: defeat.

Q: *You seem to trivialize defeat. Doesn't winning matter at all?*

A: Of course winning matters. Winning is the object of every race. It's perfectly healthy to want to swim faster than anyone else. Positive striving (actively pursuing goal-attainment) is important. What matters is the pursuit of victory, not the isolated moment of winning. It's the process within which the value lies, not the product. Winning as the object of the quest in competitive swimming enhances the value of the chase.

Since it is the goal of the game, victory can be a cause for celebration. Defeat may be cause for temporary disappointment. You are not however, a better person if you win, nor a less worthwhile person if you get beat.

Remember there are no punishing consequences for losing *structured* into the sport of swimming. Getting beat is only aversive because most of us tend to torture ourselves when we do poorly. We don't need to do that.

The sport does not require us to get fined, flogged or put in jail if we lose. The last place finisher doesn't get bamboo under her finger nails. There may be rewards for the winners, but there are no adverse consequences delivered contingent upon losing a swimming race.

There is a big difference between missing the opportunity to get something good, and getting something bad. In a swimming race, you may miss a desired reward, but even when you swim poorly you receive no punishment. A missed opportunity is not worthy of major upset. Even when you lose, at worst, you come away no worse off than you began; while you ought to be richer for the quest.

Q: *You mentioned that it may be worthwhile to examine defeat as a method of guiding future action. Would different sets of goals change the way one looks at defeat?*

A: Yes. Defeat may or may not have relevance to your personal goals. For example, I have many interrelated goals for my participation in Masters swimming. I want to win. If I don't win, I want to beat as many people as possible. I want to improve my times, my race strategies, and my techniques. I want to swim fast. I want to stay healthy and fit. I want to enjoy my swimming.

In my case, I see all these goals as supportive of each other. I enjoy striving for improvement because it increases my chances of winning. Making my swimming fun enhances my swimming performance. I find striving for victory makes swimming more fun; which helps me to train harder; which keeps me healthier and more fit, and promotes improvement; all of which helps me to win. I can't lose.

For me, it makes sense to take stock of how I did after each race in order to decide what I can do to improve because I want to win the next time. Take note however, that as much as I strive for victory, it's the quest I enjoy. I don't like getting beat. There have been races I enjoyed immensely however, in which I either got touched out, creamed or both. I would have much preferred to have won, but they were still fun.

For someone, who is swimming purely for fitness or recreation, defeat is irrelevant; not even worthy of the fleeting glance I strive to give it. Think about it. What if, after the fact, you didn't concern yourself at all with the result of the race? What if, after you swam, you responded to queries of "how did you do?" with "I had fun!"?

There Aren't Any Speed Limits

Throughout the 1981 NCAA Swimming and Diving Championships, people kept coming up to me and asking me if I thought there were limits to how fast an event could be swim. After all, there had been ten American Records broken in the three day meet and some of them were shattered. Surely there is a limit to how fast swimmers could swim? Or, so I was asked.

Well, I'm not sure. It stands to reason that there probably are some limits to how fast an event can be swum. It's extremely difficult to imagine a zero second 50 freestyle. Nevertheless, we do not know what the limits are. I think it is highly unlikely that we have reached them. I know it's not useful to think that we have!

There are so many factors (heredity, training, outlook, etc.) that go into determining the level of performance that there's bound to be room for further improvement. I doubt that we ever have seen an optimally-prepared-for, perfect swim.

There is no question but that heredity, physical preparation, and strategy largely determine how fast you swim. Nevertheless, the way you train is greatly influenced by what you think is possible. If you limit what you think is possible, you limit what you do to prepare. Moreover, given whatever preparation you have done by race time, the limitations to meet performances are largely psychological.

You have to be open to the prospect of phenomenal feats. There is no use limiting performances with too targeted goals or other psychological barriers.

Goals are tremendously useful. For one thing, they provide you with something for which to shoot. They create the game. They can however, serve to target your efforts too much, thereby limiting the level of performance. That's why I recommend open-ended goals that place no limits on performance; goals to swim *at least* as fast as some time and as far under that designated standard as possible.

People tend to zero in on some number and make it into too tough a psychological barrier. And, what artificial barriers they are! In the past, a four minute 400m. freestyle, a one minute 100m. backstroke, and a two minute 200m. butterfly have all been tough barriers to break. They have however, been broken. Similarly, until recently the two minute mark for the 200 breaststroke seemed like a milestone, but when you think about it there is no noticeable difference in actual time between 2:00.00 and 1:59.99, except on paper. Well, after many swimmers knocked on the door, Steve Lundquist finally broke the "magic two minute barrier." Now, six people went under two minutes at NCAAs. Meanwhile, Steve went 1:55.01; and he sure looked as though he could have gone faster.

Steve's swim was only one among many performances at this year's NCAAs which prompted talk of limits and psychological barriers. Bill Barrett's 1:45.01 200yd. I.M., Robin Leamy's 19:36 50 yd. freestyle, Steve Lundquist's :52.93 100yd. breaststroke as well as his 1:55.01 200yd. swim, Rowdy Gaines' :42.38 100yd. freestyle and his :41.48 relay split, and the University of Texas' 3:12.93 Medley Relay all got people talking.

Richard Quick was telling us that "Rowdy is free from psychological barriers," while 50 freestyle champion, Texas' Kris Kirchner, was suggesting, "it's not how fast you go, it's how fast you think." Florida's John Hillencamp (2nd in the 500yd. freestyle) sported a "No Limits" t-shirt.

The importance of unlimiting yourself cannot be overemphasized. Be unlimited in your thinking and in your actions. There may be limits. Who knows? But there is no use in thinking that there are. Certainly, there is no use in thinking that you have reached your limits.

Breath-Taking Pressure

It was the Olympic Trials. Scott Spann was ready. He felt as though he had prepared better for this one meet, this one race, than he ever had prepared for anything in his entire career. Everything was perfect — or so it seemed.

Scott exploded off the start of the 100 meter butterfly as only he can do. Everything felt great. His stroke was smooth, efficient, and extraordinarily powerful. It quickly carried him to a sizeable lead. But the lead wouldn't last.

Q: *What happened?*

A: Well, as Scott told me, "I was so nervous I lost my feel. I dove in. I had my best start. Everything was perfect. But I was so totally absorbed in my race that I forgot to breathe! I didn't take a breath until after 25 meters. It never occurred to me [to breathe]. Even when I finally thought about it at 25 meters, I didn't feel like I needed it, but I told myself I had to breathe. When I came off the turn at 50 meters — all of a sudden, it was like a ton of bricks hit me."

Even though Scott was "possibly as nervous as I've ever been," he had it pretty well under control. For the most part he was using the nervousness in a healthy way. He viewed his physiological arousal as eager anticipation and got excited. He felt confident as he reminded himself of how well-prepared he was, physically and psychologically. But nervousness can lead to a narrowing of attentional focus. It can be distracting. In this case, it led to Scott's forgetting to breathe.

Q: *What would get someone like Scott Spann — a National age-group record-holder, three time NCAA champion and All American, Kiphuth award winner and former American Record holder — that nervous? What makes anyone nervous?*

A: It could be any of a number of things; all of them related to some perceived threat. In the Olympic Trials, it was making the outcome of one race overly precious that made Scott anxious. He recalls viewing that moment as if, "I had 17 years of my life laid on the line in one race." Talk about pressure. That's a pretty heavy load to carry.

Q: *What else causes anxiety?*

A: Scott says that the main thing that gets him nervous is "fear of failure." "Whether it's fear of not winning the race, fear of failure to deal with the oncoming pain, or fear of not being able to meet a goal I have set for myself. The more my fear of failure is in force, the more nervous I get."
        Actually the prospect of failing isn't the real culprit. If you fail, you fail. Sure that's disappointing. You may miss an opportunity to reap the rewards of victory and the pleasure of doing well. But the prospect of a little disappointment is not that scary. What's scary is thinking that *you are a failure if you fail.*
        In fact, most performance anxiety stems from viewing performance as reflective of personal worth. If you think of yourself as a failure, if you fail to reach your goals; if you think of yourself as no good, if you swim poorly; then you tend to fear failure. It's when your ego seems to be on the line that you get apprehensive about the outcome of your performance.

It doesn't matter whether it is the Olympic Trials, Masters Nationals, a small local Masters meet, or a time trial. The prospect of not performing well is certainly unpleasant. It only becomes a threat however, if you rate your *Self* based on how well you perform.

One swimmer recently described to me his reflections upon competing in his first Masters meet. (For that matter, it was his first swim meet of any kind.)

"I had horror story pictures in my mind of drowning halfway through the race. I flashed back to a big music festival in High School where I was playing a trumpet solo and really blew the piece. I had to stop in front of my contemporaries. I wanted to avoid a replay of that kind of abysmal failure."

"I want to best at least minimum ability level when I do things in front of other people. I had some expectations of what I should do. That added a bit of self-imposed pressure which distracted me from thinking about the race and what I should be doing."

Assuming that you need to swim at a certain level of competence in order to feel okay about yourself, as this swimmer did, produces anxiety. Even if you've set reasonable standards for competent performances, the prospect of not feeling okay about yourself, if you fail to reach them, can be scary.

There is nothing wrong with feeling disappointed in your swim when you fail to meet your standards. There is a big difference however, between feeling disappointed in your performance when you don't swim well and feeling disappointed in yourself.

Unreasonable expectations readily set you up for failure. If you demand that you perform at standards at which you cannot reasonably expect to perform given your level of preparedness, you set yourself up for failure and an impending poor self-rating.

Heidi Ernst, who in 1979 had the fastest times in the 100m., 200m., and 400m. freestyle for women in the 25 to 29 age group, had some possibly unreasonable expectations contribute to her apprehension about getting into Masters swimming.

"I thought it would get me nervous to have to face the comparison between the times I did before and what I could do now," she told me. Apparently, she felt as if she had to swim as fast as she had in her senior swimming heyday in order to feel okay about herself. She felt reasonably sure she couldn't match those performances on the amount of training she was putting in as a Masters swimmer.

Q: *Shouldn't I care about how well I swim?*

A: Of course you should care about how well you swim. It is useful to care. If you didn't care, you may forever be swimming in mediocrity. (Yes, I mean that both ways.) It is the quest for achievement of personal goals that brings much of the enjoyment and, of course, the speed into swimming. If you don't care, you may not strive for any goals. It's just not useful however, to be concerned, to worry.

Worry permeates anxiety. Worry is outcome-oriented. It does nothing to help you prepare, plan and rehearse for the very performance that determines the outcome about which you worry.

Q: *Okay, I have a pretty good understanding of some of the things that contribute to anxiety, but how do I cope with it?*

A: Some nervousness is natural and not necessarily bad. Put it to work for you. Don't let it work against you.

A little nervousness is really nothing about which to be concerned. Worrying about being nervous only makes it worse.

Jim Crane, 1980 35-39 Masters National Champion in the 500yd., 1650yd., 200m., 400m. and 1500m. freestyles, says he sometimes gets nervous before a race, but "I don't worry about it because I know it's going to go away when I get in the water."

Use the nervousness as a signal to relax. You can't be relaxed and anxious at the same time.

Scott Spann says that he often employs the relaxation techniques I've shown him. He says, "if I find myself getting too nervous, I take a few deep breaths and concentrate on relaxing every muscle in my body."

The most important thing is to keep the proper perspective. While sometimes there are rewards for performing well and often a great deal of pleasure, there is really nothing to lose by swimming poorly. Don't put your ego on the line. A race is an opportunity to see how well you can do, not how good you are.

Remember why you are competing. Know your priorities.

Heidi Ernst finally got over her apprehension. She has been enjoying swimming Masters ever since. "It took me a long time to realize that it is more important to continue swimming than to go fast," she said. "I'd like to keep swimming for the rest of my life. That's more important than fast times."

Heidi went on to observe, "there's not much pressure in Masters. It's never a one-time thing like the Olympic Trials. There's always another chance."

Heidi is right. Masters swimming need not present any pressure — just a lifetime of opportunities.

The Night Before

You've been training all year for tomorrow's meet. You can hardly contain your excitement. The anticipation swells up inside until you feel as though you may explode. And, why not? This is going to be fun. The big meets are much of what it is all about.

You're nervous. It's all-your-eggs-in-one-basket time. You've trained hours upon hours for months in preparation for this one chance. Now the moment is about to arrive.

Couple the excitement and nervousness with a well-rested, finely-honed body that yearns to be used and there's no wonder you're having difficulty getting to sleep. Heck! Merely lying still can be a challenge.

Images of the meet flash through your mind. The pool and its surroundings, your competitors, and critical points in your race all emerge and disappear with lightning speed.

Your body can't help but respond to these images. You want to get some sleep, but your body's awfully keyed up and your head keeps working overtime.

You've tried plugging in the relaxation skills you've been developing. You've found relaxation to be a tremendous boon to calming down a reved-up body.

You've also found that imaginally employing a peaceful scene (like going to the beach in your head) will calm you down and temporarily distract you from your thoughts of the upcoming meet. But as soon as your attention drifts from the relaxation, your thoughts return to the meet.

It would be nice to put tomorrow's competition out of your mind and go to sleep, but you can't stop thinking about it. Then it occurs to you to stop fighting it. You think, "why not take control, make good use of what is already occuring naturally and effortlessly, and carry it to its logical conclusion?"

"Instead of letting your mind wander where it may, with the risk of filling your head with doubts, fears, or even vivid images of failure; why not use this relentless barrage of thoughts and images to prepare yourself better for the meet? Why not use the recognition that you're having trouble keeping your mind off of the meet as a signal — a reminder — to take control and guide your thoughts and images to some positive use?"

So you take control. You intentionally picture yourself arriving at the pool and calmly, comfortably, confidently familiarizing yourself with the surroundings.

You picture yourself warming up with a purpose (familiarizing yourself with the pool and getting your body loose and accustomed to effort) rather than using warm-up as a test of how you feel and worrying about it. You visualize yourself acting confident; accepting any nervous anticipation as a natural sign that you are in the midst of an exciting meet in which you seek to do well. You use the mild uneasiness as a signal to relax.

You see yourself approaching the blocks calmly; focusing on what you will do; aware of a few key things you want to remember; and ready to explode.

You feel yourself calmly building into the race, fully in control. Your stroke feels smooth, fast, efficient, and relaxed. You feel yourself powerfully gliding through the water. You hear the air bubbles sizzling past your ears. You feel yourself meeting the challenge presented by fatigue and conquering it: accepting the sensations, relaxing and going fast — faster than you've ever gone before!

You experience the exhiliration of a strong finish, concluding your best-ever performance. You thrill at your success.

Then you allow the momentary excitement to fade into a calm, peaceful satisfaction. You quietly make your way to the warm-up pool and swim down. Gently riding an easy stroke across the water, you cleanse your body of the aftereffects of a fast swim; all the while lost in the good feeling you have about your race.

When you feel fully recovered, you head for the shower. There you feel the spray of the warm water gently massaging your body.

After drying off, you find yourself sitting on the bench in the locker room, relaxing. You imagine yourself feeling satisfied, pleased, at peace and completely relaxed as you fade off into a gentle — peaceful — rejuvenating — extremely restful — sleep.

What If I Don't Make Cuts?

"What if I don't make cuts?" A thought that can wreak terror in the minds of swimmers young and old.

"What if I don't make cuts?" A subvocal rhetorical statement of great interest and great irony.

When you ask yourself: "What if I don't make cuts?" it doesn't really send you on a cognitive search for the possible consequences of failing to attain qualifying standards in your upcoming swim. "What if I don't make cuts?" is a rhetorical question, a statement disguised as a question. The implicit message varies in form, but says something like: "I'm not going to make cuts." "When I fail to make cuts, it is going to be terrible and I won't be able to stand it" (meaning, of course, that "I'm going to die," either literally or figuratively, from the embarassment of having failed; from the letdown of missing the opportunity; from the now, clearly-demonstrated proof that I am a lesser human being for having failed in my quest; or from the emptiness of a life newly devoid of purpose).

"What if I don't make cuts?" brings these imagined, dire consequences into sharp focus exactly when they can do the most harm. The anxiety wrought by these anticipated consequences plays a major role in making this rhetorical statement a self-fulfilling prophecy.

Ironic, isn't it? By worrying about the anticipated prospect of failing to make qualifying standards, one tends to generate anxiety, which, in turn, interupts the relaxed, focused, energized flow that feeds peak performances. Worrying about failing to make cuts makes you more likely to fail to make cuts.

But what if you don't make cuts? Well, the true consequences are those of missed opportunity. Miss cuts and you don't get to swim in the next, more exclusive meet that constitutes the pyramided structure of the sport of competitive swimming. Miss cuts for the state championships and you don't get to swim in the state championships. Miss cuts for Jr. Nationals and you don't get to swim in Jr. Nationals. Miss cuts for Nationals and you don't get to swim in Nationals. Miss cuts for the Olympic Trials and you don't get to swim in the Olympic Trials. Miss making the finals or finishing in the top designated places and you don't make the Olympic Team: meaning you don't get to swim in the Olympics. Miss making the finals in the Olympics and you don't get to swim in the Olympic final. Then, of course, you can't win the Olympics.

I guess missing the opportunity to win the Olympics is a missed opportunity of more than passing importance to most swimmers. But then a closer examination of the likely consequences of such a passing of events is quite interesting. Winning the Olympics probably is a truly extraordinary, individually-meaningful experience. I wouldn't know personally. I missed that opportunity. My wife however, did not. She won three gold medals in the 1972 Olympics. Near as I can tell, those experiences are quite special to her, they mean a lot. But other than the fact that every life event seems to shape our future world, I'm not sure her gold medals generate that much practical significance. Hell, I know how much they are worth. They are pretty. They evoke warm, exciting memories in Sandy and seem to evoke similar feelings in others, at least in terms of what might have been, what may someday be, or empathic, vicarious, warm fuzzies. But they are not worth much money. (In fact, they cost her $25.00/year in rent on the safe deposit box at the bank in which she keeps them.) One has to be quite creative to play with them. And one can't eat them. They are merely symbols reminding her of how much fun it was to race.

Fortunately, we are currently entering an era where there finally may be financial gain and career opportunities for swimmers reaching the pinnacle of success. It seems that Matt Biondi may be the first American to be earning a living by swimming. But for the time being, for most, making cuts opens few, if any, doors. Making cuts merely provides an opportunity to swim in another, future, albeit more exclusive, swimming meet.

Yes, meets with qualifying standards have a certain amount of exclusivity. That's the point of cuts. The upshoot of which is that the competition is tough, the challenge substantial. Of course, if you find yourself swimming in a meet where there remains serious doubt as to whether or not you can make cuts, isn't the challenge at hand substantial?

I've always thought it careless that swimmers get so focused on the meet for which they are trying to make cuts that they fail to value the very meet which provides the opportunity to make cuts, the only opportunity to race that presently lies before them. Make cuts, and you get to swim in another challenging meet. But isn't the immediate opportunity to swim challenging? Why is the exclusive meet necessarily better? Isn't there excitement in the focused utilization of all your preparation now needed if you are to make cuts?

The greatest irony, of course, being that the more you worry about making cuts, the harder it is to make them. The more you embrace the opportunity at hand and stay focused on the moment, the more likely it is that you will have fun, swim fast, and make cuts; thereby earning another opportunity to race.

But then, so what if you don't make cuts? Isn't there always another swimming meet, another opportunity to race?

Hold On To What You've Got

The Summer Season is just coming to an end. Most teams are laying off for anywhere from a couple of weeks to a few months.

There is no question but that most coaches can use some time off. Coaches maintain an incredibly harried schedule: start coaching before dawn, work into the evening and often put in twelve hour days on weekends at meets. For the swimmers however, it's another matter.

Not that swimmers don't put in the hours. They do. And those long, hours can be quite demanding. But that's demanding play. Swimming is fun. It's healthful. And there is much to be said for continuity of training.

Competitive swimming may not offer some of the incentives other sports do. Certainly the money isn't there. Nor is the recognition as likely or as great. But as a lifetime program for health, fitness and recreation, competitive swimming can't be beat. When we treat swimming as a seasonal sport however, we chip away at swimming's very foundation of greatness. Extended layoffs are not conducive to a lifetime sport. We ought to be encouraging a program of continued, regular exercise.

Between seasons may be a good time to ease up on intensity, distance, and the time demands of the high levels of training commitment otherwise needed to pursue excellence. This may be a good time to do some of the other things you may not have the time or energy to do during the peak of training. But during the break in the competitive season, swim. Swim for pleasure and maintenance of conditioning, if not for a competitive advantage.

Consider swimming two to four thousand meters at least three or four times a week as a maintenance program. If you've been going twelve to twenty thousand six or seven days per week during the peak of the season, you will have lots of time and energy for other life experiences.

My idea of a break is to do a little less yardage and perhaps to do it somewhat less intensely. (I say "perhaps" because I usual find myself "getting after it" even when I've planned only to cruise a few thousand. It's fun to swim fast. I enjoy challenging my body and challenging the clock.)

Even during a break, my personal preference is to swim seven days per week. I find that a day without swimming is missing something. I feel all wet when I'm out of the water. Swimming is not only a habit, part of my daily routine, but it is a nice part of the day; something to which I look forward.

You don't need to swim seven days per week like I do. But a lifetime sport should be part of your daily routine at least three or four days per week, even during "layoffs." Maintaining a high level of fitness is healthier and more fun.

Moreover, it is hard to get in shape. It's hard psychologically and it's hard on your body. It's easy however, to maintain conditioning.

Everytime you get out of shape and have to start all over it can take some of the fun out of it. What better way to get discouraged or burned out then to start from scratch at least two times a year, not being able to handle the work loads, let alone go fast?

The higher the level of your performance, the harder it is to make your way back up to the top. You got to the top by putting in that little bit extra. If you let it all slide, you have a longer way to go to recapture that winning edge. Why start all over?

Swimming is much more fun when you can do it well enough to challenge yourself, when your goals seem meaningful. While it is true that you can set challenging goals at whatever is your present level of conditioning, the contextual nature of having had more challenging goals in the past, tends to make it difficult to value lesser goals. It is more difficult to maintain a continuing interest and commitment to an activity that is only moderately engaging. It is tough to get excited about holding a series of 100's at a minute, if two months ago you could hold a similar set of 100's at :55. Getting back in shape tends to feel more like paying your dues than meeting the challenge.

Swimming should be something to which you look forward, not something that has to be done. Don't take time off from your training, time off sounds like being out on parole and implies that training is like imprisonment.

Yes, back off from the intensity once in a while. The rest will do you good.

Take time for your family, friends, and other activities. They too are important.

But take care of your level of fitness. Protect the skills and conditioning that make the game so much more fun to play.

P.S.

It poured today. While I sat at the computer typing, I listened to the pounding rain. The sound of water dropping from the sky formed a concerto, both soothing and arousing. It evoked the kind of relaxed, exhilirating feelings that foster swimming fast.

Though I was deeply lost in my editing, my hunger finally broke through loudly enough to strongly suggest a lunch break. Besides, I would want my lunch to settle some before heading off for an early afternoon swim.

As I walked into the living room, I could hear Sandy telling our one-year-old son, Cooper, "go tell Daddy that you want to go out into the rain."

Cooper is just beginning to talk. His receptive vocabularly far exceeds his expressive vocabularly, but words weren't necessary. Cooper ran over to me, stopped, pointed outside, and turned and excitedly ran to the sliding glass door.

Following Cooper to the door, I slid it open for him. Like a swimmer exploding off the starting block almost simultaneously with the horn, as the glass obstacle was moved out of the way Cooper was unleashed. He burst smoothly onto our back porch and into the rain.

Clad only in his diaper, he stood there for a moment as the cold drops splattered down on him, his rain-speckled face breaking through a look of expected bewilderment with an excited smile. Then, as the smile triumphed, he scampered into the yard through the grass, mud, and puddles. Running back and forth in the rain he carommed from wet rock to puddle to knee-deep grass like a pinball from the bumpers. His giggles drowned out the rain's concerto, while his laughter and his smile lit up the overcast sky.

We stood frozen to this scene as our boy stomped down on the puddles, kicking up the water, then pushed his way on through this natural, water amusement park. He stopped, bent over a puddle and blew bubbles, as he's been learning to do in the pool and the bathtub. But that couldn't last too long. The excitement was too great and there was too much more to experience this morning running free in the spring storm.

His speed built with his continual excitement until newly-learned ambulatory skills couldn't keep up the pace. He lost his balance mid-stride at peak speed and belly-flopped smack dab in the center of the largest puddle in the back yard. Bouncing up like one of those plastic punching bags, he paused only long enough to look over at us and gleefully laugh out loud before immediately returning to his romp in the backyard arcade that had been created by the rain.

I don't know how long he played out there; my awareness was totally devoid of time as we watched him frolic in the water. I do know that he never stopped. Rather, suspecting that he must be getting extremely cold and not wanting him to get sick, we wrapped a towel around him and carried him inside. Cooper resisted. His screams, flailing arms, and kicking legs violently protested our decision.

His unmitigated joy, eminating from his movements, his expression, and the sound of his laughter, was clearly apparent as we watched him in the storm. When we brought him in out of the rain, he didn't have the words to tell us, but even at his tender age, he had no trouble making his feelings abundantly clear: having to come in out of the water felt all wet.

References

BANDURA, ALBERT. *Principles of Behavior Modification.* New York: Holt, Rinehart and Winston, 1969.

BANDURA, ALBERT. *Social Learning Theory.* Englewood Cliffs, New Jersey: Prentice-Hall, 1977.

BELL, KEITH F. "A cognitive approach to enhancing performance and enjoyment." Chapter in *Golf Psychology*, Frazier, Claude A. (Ed.).

BELL, KEITH F. "Bad Pain . . . Good Pain." *Running.* 1982, Vol. 8, No. 2, p. 10 & 11.

BELL, KEITH F. *Championship Sports Psychology.* Austin, Texas: Keel Publications, 1990.

BELL, KEITH F. *Coaching Excellence.* Austin, Texas: Keel Publications, 1985.

BELL, KEITH F. "Psychology and Coaching: Extended Layoffs." *Coach.* 1980, Vol. 2, No. 4, p. 37.

BELL, KEITH F. "Psychology and Swimming: Education Aids Motivation." *Swimmers.* 1981, Vol. 3, No. 7, p. 28.

BELL, KEITH F. "Psychology and Swimming: Just Making It." *Swimmers.* 1979, Vol. 2, No. 5, pp. 52-53.

BELL, KEITH F. "Psychology and Swimming: On Excuses, Rejected Compliments, Public Anger and Fear of Failure." *Swimmers.* 1980, Vol. 3, No. 3, pp. 25 & 28.

BELL, KEITH F. "Psychology and Swimming: Pain Management." *Swimmers.* 1980, Vol. 3, No. 2, pp. 18-19.

BELL, KEITH F. "Psychology and Swimming: Perceived Disadvantage." *Swimmers.* 1980, Vol. 3, No. l, pp. 16-17.

BELL, KEITH F. "Psychology and Swimming: Plateaus." *Swimmers.* 1980, Vol. 3, No. 4, p. 37.

BELL, KEITH F. "Psychology and Swimming: Relaxation For Maximum Speed." *Swimmers.* 1981, Vol. 4, No. 2, pp. 11 & 15.

BELL, KEITH F. "Psychology and Swimming: The Language of Winning Swimming." *Swimmers.* 1980, Vol. 3, No. 5, p. 17.

BELL, KEITH F. "Psychology and Swimming: The Night Before." *Swimmers.* 1981, Vol. 4, No. 4, p. 30.

BELL, KEITH F. "Psychology and Swimming: The Self-Image Fairy Tale." *Swimmers.* 1980, Vol. 3, No. 6, pp. 22 & 32.

BELL, KEITH F. "Psychology and Swimming: What Might Have Been." *Swimmers.* 1979, Vol. 2, No. 6, pp. 39-40.

BELL, KEITH F. "Psychology and Swimming: Where Are The Limits?" *Swimmers.* 1981, Vol. 4, No. 2, pp. 11 & 15.

BELL, KEITH F. "Relaxation training for competitive swimming." *Swimming Technique.* 1976, Vol. 13, No. 2, pp. 41-43.

BELL, KEITH F. "Self-instructional methods." *Swimmers Coach.* 1979, Vol. 1, No. 1, pp. 29-32.

BELL, KEITH F. "Sports Psychology: Building a Good Attitude." *SWIM.* 1989, Vol. V, No. 1, pp. 23-24.

BELL, KEITH F. "Sports Psychology: Commitment." *SWIM* 1989, Vol. V, No. 4, p. 12.

BELL, KEITH F. "Sports Psychology: For All the Right Reasons." *SWIM.* 1989, Vol. V, No. 2, pp.13-14.

BELL, KEITH F. "Swimming Psychology: Controlling for confidence." *SWIM SWIM.* 1981, Vol. 3, No. 4, pp. 9 & 93.

BELL, KEITH F. "Swimming Psychology: Losing." *SWIM SWIM.* 1982, Vol. 4, No. 2, p. 11.

BELL, KEITH F. "Swimming Psychology: Motivation for Lifetime Swimming." *SWIM SWIM*. 1981, Vol. 3, No. 1, pp. 8 & 29.

BELL, KEITH F. "Swimming Psychology: Removing the Pressure." *SWIM SWIM*. 1981, Vol. 3, No. 2, pp. 13 & 64.

BELL, KEITH F. "Swimming Psychology: Shortcuts to Success." *SWIM SWIM*. 1982, Vol. 4, No. 4, p. 9.

BELL, KEITH F. "Swimming Psychology: So What?" *SWIM SWIM*. 1982, Vol. 4, No. 3, pp. 11 & 64.

BELL, KEITH F. "Swimming Psychology: Working Out Alone." *SWIM SWIM*. 1981, Vol. 3, No. 3, pp. 9 & 94.

BELL, KEITH F. *Target on Gold: Goal Setting for Swimmers and Other Kinds of People*. Austin, Texas: Keel Publications, 1983.

BELL, KEITH F. *The Nuts and Bolts of Psychology for Swimmers*. Austin, Texas: Keel Publications, 1980.

BELL, KEITH F. *Winning Isn't Normal*. Austin, Texas: Keel Publications, 1982.

BENSON, HERBERT. *The Relaxation Response*. New York: Morrow, 1975.

MEICHENBAUM, DONALD. *Cognitive Behavior Modification*. Morristown, New Jersey: General Learning Press, 1974.

MEICHENBAUM, DONALD. "Self-Instructional Methods." A chapter in *Helping People Change*, by Kanfer, F. H. and Goldstein, A. P. (Eds.). Pergamon Press, 1974, 357-392.

SCHOLLANDER, DON and DUKE SAVAGE. *Deep Water*. New York: Crown, 1971.

SWIMMING WORLD, 1976, Vol 17 (9).

VELTEN, EMMETT JR. "A laboratory task for induction of mood states." In Goldfried, Marvin R. and Merbaum, Michael (Eds.). *Behavior Control Through Self-Control*. New York: Holt, Rinehart and Winston, 1973.

WOLPE, JOSEPH and ARNOLD A. LAZARUS. *Behavior Therapy Techniques: A Guide to the Treatment of Neuroses*. New York: Pergamon, 1966.

About The Author

Dr. Keith Bell is an internationally known sports psychologist, coach and athlete. He received his Ph.D. in 1974 from the University of Texas. Since then, he has helped thousands of coaches and athletes perform better and enjoy their sport more through his seminars, speaking engagements, consultations and publications.

Dr. Bell has coached NCAA, club and masters swimming teams, runners and triathletes. In 1988 he was named United States Masters Swimming Coach of the Year. An NCAA, masters and long-distance All-American swimmer, Dr. Bell has won numerous World and National swimming titles. He presently ranks among the fastest masters swimmers in the world.

Other Books by Dr. Keith Bell:

- PSYCHOLOGY FOR SWIMMERS
- CHAMPIONSHIP SPORTS PSYCHOLOGY
- WINNING ISN'T NORMAL
- GOAL SETTING FOR SWIMMERS:
         and Other Kinds of People.
- COACHING EXCELLENCE

Did you borrow this book? If so, why not order one for yourself?

┌──────────────────── ORDER FORM ────────────────────┐

Please send me the following books by Dr. Keith Bell:

____ copies of The Nuts & Bolts of **PSYCHOLOGY FOR SWIMMERS** . @ $11.95

____ copies of **CHAMPIONSHIP SPORTS PSYCHOLOGY** . . . . @ $21.95

____ copies of **WINNING ISN'T NORMAL** . . . . @ $10.95

____ copies of **GOAL SETTING FOR SWIMMERS:**
     and Other Kinds of People . . . . @ $ 8.95

____ copies of **COACHING EXCELLENCE** . . . . @ $19.95

____ copies of **YOU ONLY FEEL WET**
     WHEN YOU'RE OUT OF THE WATER:
     Thoughts on Psychology and Competitive Swimming . . . @ $16.95

All prices subject to change without notice

NAME _____

ADDRESS _____

*CITY*_____*STATE* _____*ZIP* _____

Shipping: Please include $2.00 for the first book ($3.50 for orders outside the
     U.S.A.) and 75¢ for each additional book ordered. For Air Mail within
     the U.S.A. please include $3.75 per book.

Sales Tax: Please add 6.25% sales tax for every book shipped to a Texas address.

Enclosed please find a check or money order for total of $_____ .
(For orders outside U.S.A. please remit an international money order payable in US$.)
Please make payable to:

     KEEL PUBLICATIONS
     P.O. Box 160155
     Austin, Texas 78716
     (512) 327-1280

└───┘

Please allow 4–6 weeks for delivery.